Date Due			

The Rehearsal

A Play in Three Acts

by

JEAN ANOUILH

English Version

by

PAMELA HANSFORD JOHNSON

and

KITTY BLACK

SAMUEL FRENCH

LONDON

NEW YORK   TORONTO   SYDNEY   HOLLYWOOD

THE REHEARSAL

Produced by Tennent Productions Ltd in association with the Bristol Old Vic Company, at The Globe Theatre, London, on the 6th April 1961, with the following cast of characters:

(in the order of their appearance)

A FOOTMAN, the Count's valet	*Andrew Kane*
M. DAMIENS, the Countess's lawyer	*Lockwood West*
THE COUNTESS	*Phyllis Calvert*
THE COUNT, her husband	*Robert Hardy*
HORTENSIA, the Count's mistress	*Diana Churchill*
HERO, the Count's friend	*Alan Badel*
VILLEBOSSE, the Countess's lover	*Jeremy Burnham*
LUCILE, M. Damiens's god-daughter	*Maggie Smith*

Directed by JOHN HALE
Designed by JANE GRAHAM

SYNOPSIS OF SCENES

The action of the Play passes in the Château de Ferbroques, France, during the Spring of 1950

ACT I

SCENE 1   The Salon. Late afternoon
SCENE 2   The same. The following afternoon

ACT II

The same. The following afternoon

ACT III

SCENE 1   Lucile's small attic bedroom. The same night
SCENE 2   The Salon. The following morning

The Players are rehearsing an amateur production of Marivaux's "The Double Inconstancy" and wear Louis the Fifteenth costumes

ACT I

Scene 1

Scene—*The salon of the Château de Ferbroques, France. Late afternoon in the spring of 1950.*

It is a "conservatory" room overlooking the château grounds, with large oval skylights and long windows almost filling the back wall and the up-stage sections of the walls R *and* L. *There are entrances* R, *down* R, *and down* L. *Built-in low stone urns are in front of the upstage windows* R *and* L. *A tall climbing plant grows in the urn* R *and a grape vine grows in the urn* L. *In front of the window back* C, *there is a high stone pedestal with a large vase containing ferns, etc. In front of the pedestal stands a square black wood and gilt inlaid table. A gold and green marble console table is set against the wall below the door down* L. *A large gilt-framed mirror hangs on the wall over the console table. A wooden framed, blue-seated settee stands down* RC, *facing down* L. *An upright chair, with a blue, upholstered seat is down* R, *below the door. A small grey upholstered and gilt armchair stands* L *of the chair down* R. *A second upright, blue-seated chair is* L *of the armchair. A high-backed, carved black wooden chair is set in front of the window back* R. *An upright, blue-seated chair is set at an angle facing down* R, *in front of the pillar* L.

When the Curtain *rises, the settee is covered by a dust cover. A high-backed, carved chair is standing on the table up* C. *On the table, under the chair there is a black and gold, stiff-covered prompt script of the play in rehearsal. On the chair up* R *there is a large oval silver tray with glasses, decanters of brandy and sherry, an ashtray, and a box with cigarettes and matches. On the table down* L *there are four small paper-covered scripts and an ashtray and matches.* Monsieur Damiens *is standing up* L, *script in hand, studying his lines. The* Footman *enters down* R, *carrying an upright, blue-seated chair. He crosses and sets the chair by the table down* L. *He then crosses to the settee, removes the dust cover, folds it and puts it over the back of the settee.* Damiens *moves and looks in the mirror down* L. *The* Footman *goes to the armchair down* R *and swings it into a new place* R *of the settee. He then goes to the table up* C, *lifts down the chair from it and sets the chair* L *of the table. He puts the prompt script from the table on to the chair. He then goes to the chair up* R, *picks up the tray of drinks and puts it on the table up* C. Damiens *crosses below the settee to up* R *of it, still studying his lines. The* Footman *moves the chair* L *of the table up* C, *with the prompt script on it and sets it up* L *in the window. He then crosses to the settee. The* Countess *enters and crosses to* L *of the settee. She carries a rose. The* Footman *bows to the Countess, picks up the dust sheet, crosses and exits down* L.

COUNTESS. Monsieur Damiens, I must thank you most sincerely for lending us your goddaughter.

DAMIENS. To oblige you, madame, is the first and most pleasant of my duties. You had need of her: so it was most natural that she should come to Ferbroques.

COUNTESS. What would have become of us without her? My husband's aunt, the late Marquise, was the most whimsical creature alive. The idea of leaving us the château on condition that we spent a month here every spring, was touching enough. (*She crosses to* L, *glances in the mirror then moves up* C) She herself could never endure more than a week here. However, a month in the country, providing you give a ball or two, passes quickly enough. And how could we reject Ferbroques? It is a jewel. But the clause in the will, enjoining us to bring up twelve orphan children in the west wing, must have given her great satisfaction when she wrote it.

DAMIENS. Perhaps a concern for Christian charity . . . ?

COUNTESS (*moving behind the settee*) My husband's aunt was a child of the Enlightenment. It would only have been sheer politeness which, on her deathbed, dictated this small gesture towards heaven. She detested children. They were a phobia with her, ever since she was hit on the head by a diabolo in a garden. (*She gestures to Damiens to sit*)

(DAMIENS *sits in the armchair* R *of the settee*)

(*She crosses to the table down* L *and puts the rose on it*) For my part, I can only see one explanation for the founding of this orphanage: the desire to play a delicious, posthumous trick on the Count and myself. Tiger, of course, took it extremely well. He adored arguing with his aunt. (*She moves up* C) "Splendid!" he cried, when the lawyer had finished. "She wants twelve scamps to deafen us one month in the year? We'll parry the thrust, my dear: we'll seek out twelve little deaf-mutes."

DAMIENS. Yet you gave up your project? I thought I heard children's voices when I came through the park?

COUNTESS (*moving behind the settee*) Yes. Unfortunately, the will specified "orphans", and when it comes to laying your hands on twelve orphaned deaf-mutes, you find it's extremely difficult. We collected twelve orphans fully equipped with vocal chords, and took refuge in the east wing. The only problem was to organize the grand Charity Ball Tiger and I decided to give for the opening of the orphanage. Tiger is quite marvellous at such things. One of the last men of our time to realize that futility must be taken quite seriously. In the course of a single night he conceived the theme of the ball, the theme of the whole entertainment. I can't tell you what it is, because it's still a great secret. In short—(*she leans over the back of the settee*) all was going well, the great day was approaching and then suddenly, one morning—disaster. The orphans arrived. We had forgotten all about them. That was when I sent you my telegram, and you were kind enough to lend us your goddaughter to help us out. I hope she's happy here?

DAMIENS. I believe so. She adores children. I have seen very little of her. Since I arrived last night, I have only had time to fit my costume and try to learn my part.

COUNTESS (*moving below the settee and sitting on it*) It was so kind of you, too, to help us at the last minute. The unexpected defection of Gontaut-Biron, who should have played Trivelin, had thrown Tiger into the depths of despair. I feared the worst.

DAMIENS. Indeed?

COUNTESS. Indeed. Tiger has the most unexpected capacity for setting store on things. Apparently he behaved marvellously in nineteen-forty, fighting on alone on the Loire when everyone else had gone off to Toulouse. He had a little cannon, more or less tied together with string, which couldn't be brought to bear properly. He held out with it against a cloud of Pomeranian grenadiers. Five hours after the Armistice, he was still blazing away, though the others were waving white flags at him and shouting through their loud-speakers that he was making himself ridiculous. The fact that France had surrendered didn't bother him in the least. But a ball in jeopardy—that's different. He'd be quite capable of killing himself.

DAMIENS. I'm honoured to think that by taking this tiny part I can spare him so painful an obligation. At twenty I had quite a little reputation as an amateur.

COUNTESS. I'm sure you still have. A lawyer never really stops playing in comedy—in tragedy, too, alas, sometimes.

(*The* FOOTMAN *enters down* L *and stands to one side of the open door. The* COUNT *enters down* L. DAMIENS *rises*)

COUNT (*crossing to* L *of the settee*) Well, do we rehearse? The play is by Marivaux. We can't make it up as we go along. (*He crosses above the settee to* R *of the armchair* RC) Where is your goddaughter, Monsieur Damiens? It's quite outrageous for those twelve little orphans to monopolize her. We need her, too, you know.

DAMIENS. She was putting them to bed, and then coming to join us.

COUNT (*patting Damiens on the back*) Be a good soul. (*He half-pushes him towards the door down* L) Go and snatch her from the claws of those twelve little horrors. We cannot begin without her.

(DAMIENS *crosses and exits down* L. *The* FOOTMAN *follows Damiens off and closes the door*)

My dear, we've made a splendid start. (*He moves to* R *of the settee*) To perform the play during dinner was a ravishing idea. (*He moves below the armchair* RC) One character gets up from the table and calls to another: they start to talk, and everyone listens, thinking they've really got something to say. Then they recognize the play. Ah, but it's too late now—it has begun. We have by-passed the moment of terror which seizes sophisticated persons when they find themselves seated before a stage full of amateurs. (*He sits in the armchair*)

COUNTESS. There's only one snag. The play is by Marivaux. Most of them won't have read it.

COUNT. All the better. They'll think I wrote it myself. Besides, you mustn't be hard on them. They're not very bright, of course. But no-one expects people of our class to produce geniuses. We're not numerically strong enough to afford such luxuries. We leave that to the crowd. All we ask of our own kind is cohesion and continuity. For several centuries we've all shown a talent in that direction. We do our best.

COUNTESS. Another snag. If they listen to the play, the food will get cold.

COUNT. That can't be helped. We always feed them too well: it will make a change. My dear, you are very pessimistic today. Besides, the supper menu can be compiled to fit the dramatic situations. I'll bring on the lobster and champagne the moment the interest flags; nothing but toothpicks in the lyrical moments to make them go through the motions of meditation. Nothing makes a man more thoughtful than trying to dislodge a shred of meat from between two molars. (*He rises and crosses above the settee to the mirror down* L) If they go through the motions, they may even arrive at a thought—by association of ideas. (*He looks in the mirror*) I think this child will be charming as Silvia.

COUNTESS. I think she lacks sparkle. I wonder why you turned everything upside down to give her the part.

COUNT (*crossing to the Countess*) That's just it. She'll be a splendid contrast to your dazzling friends. She burns with an inward fire which she cloaks under a veil of shyness. (*He crosses below the settee to* R) It will make a change from all those professional beauties who blaze like a bonfire all the evening—(*he crosses above the armchair and stands up* L *of it*) until you get them home, and then you find the fire's—dead out. Besides, for these people who call everyone by nicknames, it'll be an additional piquancy not to have the slightest idea who she is.

COUNTESS. You wouldn't, by any chance, be in love with her?

COUNT. I? Not in the least.

COUNTESS. I'm relieved to hear it.

COUNT (*looking towards the mirror*) The drawback to this Louis Quinze costume is the wig. Makes one look like a spaniel. But it must be part of my aunt's revenge—Ferbroques is an eighteenth-century château and we couldn't avoid it. (*He crosses below the settee to the mirror*) But I shan't sleep until I've thought of something to make it more amusing.

COUNTESS. How old is she?

COUNT. Just twenty. You must help me think.

COUNTESS. About what?

COUNT. The Louis Quinze costumes. We could very well drown

in banality on their account. (*He looks in the mirror*) What a hideous wig. (*He removes his wig*)

COUNTESS. Supposing we told everyone not to wear their wigs?

COUNT (*putting his wig on the chair down* L) Of course, it's much better. Particularly because the child has hair of a really exceptional colour—it would be a crime to hide it.

COUNTESS. I find her rather ugly.

COUNT. So do I. (*He crosses to the Countess*) I was speaking of the colour of her hair.

COUNTESS. You know you're quite free, Tiger. Do me the justice to admit that I have never meddled with your love affairs. Don't play the fool too much with her, all the same. Damiens has been my family solicitor for more than thirty years, and I shouldn't like him to have anything to hold against us.

COUNT. What do you take me for, my dear? I have grave faults, I know, but no-one has ever questioned my good manners. (*He crosses above the settee to* R) In fact, my manner, my coat-of-arms and my name are more or less all I can call my own if I except this château and the dozen orphans.

COUNTESS (*rising and moving up* C) That's no obstacle. (*She takes a cigarette from the box on the table up* C)

(*The* COUNT *takes a lighter from his pocket, moves to* R *of the Countess and lights her cigarette*)

COUNT. It's an obstacle to a great deal. My father, who was a most perfect man, before he died, took great care to put me on guard against that very thing. I have never forgotten it. It was a few hours before his death. (*He moves down* R) The bishop and his entire clergy were waiting in the anteroom to administer extreme unction. (*He moves to the settee and sits on it*) My father asked them to send me in first. When I was standing by the bedside, he said to me, "My boy, I have realized rather belatedly that I have never paid much attention to you. I have very little time. I'm packing my traps and Monseigneur is waiting to hear what I have to declare. So far as the family honour is concerned, I know I can trust you. As for the rest, you can rely on your instincts—it has no great importance, anyway. There is just one thing. You're young; you'll want to enjoy yourself. Always follow your own desires, but with women of your own world. With any others, it always turns out badly. Peccadilloes, if you like, my boy, none of us are angels—but in your own world. Now, send in the bishop. I must empty my bag before him and let him give me official clearance—the time has come."

(*There is a short pause. The* COUNTESS *moves behind the settee and leans on the back of it*)

(*Suddenly*) An admirable man, my father. I never got to know him, but I realized then that I loved him with my whole heart.

(*There is a short silence*)

Countess. I have the impression, Tiger—believe me, this isn't a reproach—that you really did give him your whole heart and have never given away more than a fragment of it since.

Count (*shaking himself*) My dear, how depressing your conversation is today. Besides, you know I'm extremely fond of you. I've never had such a feeling for anyone else. But don't tell Hortensia, or I shall be involved in quite another drama.

Countess (*moving down* l) Do you tell all your mistresses that you love them?

Count. One has to. Women are such sticklers for etiquette. I really believe you're the only woman to whom I have never said it.

Countess. What a singular compliment. Do you expect me to thank you? (*She shrugs*) Because it was never true.

Count. No, because there is something quite different between us, something delicate and charming, which releases me from the obligation of lying to you.

(*The* Countess *picks up her rose*)

We really must take a grip on ourselves, Eliane, or we shall become maudlin. (*He rises and crosses to the Countess*) Love is the daily bread of the poor; we cannot allow ourselves, at this late date, to sit down under our family portraits and cry our eyes out because we have never known what love is. (*He kisses her shoulder then crosses to the settee and sits on it, at the right end*)

(*The* Countess *looks in the mirror and pins the rose on her dress*)

Besides, my dear, I don't want to be indiscreet, but if you want to play at that little game, you've always got Villebosse—Villebosse or another, what do I care? The world is full of ranters and roarers.

Countess (*turning to the Count*) Villebosse bores me.

Count. I find him delightful. He's young and handsome. He is always ready to dive off the highest board, or jump through a circle of fire at the slightest provocation. You don't really expect me to sing the praises of that fellow, do you?

Countess. Be polite, Tiger. That fellow is my lover.

Count (*suddenly a little dry*) That's enough, Eliane. We're on the verge of becoming disgusting. There are some conversations I don't like. My ideas may be liberal but my words are narrow.

(*The* Countess *moves and sits* l *of the Count on the settee*)

You are free. I am free. We like each other very much, but we're here to give an entertainment, which is a real gamble in this wilderness, as you very well know. I beg you to believe there are some things infinitely more important than our little private emotions. People are never bored at our parties. With a single folly we could destroy the reputation of fifteen years in one evening. (*He rises and looks towards the mirror*) Do you really think it's better without the wig? (*He crosses to the mirror*) Yes, there's no doubt about it, you're absolutely right. There's a certain incompleteness, which makes the

Louis Quinze more endearing. (*He moves to the Countess*) You are always right. (*He kisses her hand*) I'm devoted to you, Eliane. I'll rush off instructions to everyone not to wear their wigs.

(*The* Count *exits down* r. *There is a very brief pause.*
Hortensia *enters up* r. *She carries her script*)

Hortensia. Oh, I'm sorry. They told me Tiger was with you.

Countess. He's just gone out.

Hortensia. He thinks of nothing but this ball. We never see him nowadays.

Countess (*rising and crossing to the mirror*) My dear Hortensia, I'm well past the time when I loved Tiger enough to be jealous of his parties. (*She looks in the mirror*)

Hortensia. Oh, I'm not suffering unduly. (*She moves down* rc) Are we going to rehearse? (*She looks for the place in her script*) I don't feel very sure of myself.

Countess (*turning*) That's the first time I've heard you say that.

Hortensia (*sitting on the settee, at the right end*) Acting in a comedy isn't exactly my *metier*.

Countess. Perhaps that's because the text isn't your own invention—for once. (*She moves above the settee*) We're waiting for the child who is to play Silvia.

Hortensia. Why on earth did Tiger insist on giving her the part?

Countess. She's charming.

Hortensia. I think she lacks sparkle.

Countess. You're quite wrong. She burns with an inner fire that she cloaks under a veil of shyness. (*She crosses down* r) She isn't like those dazzling young women who burn like a bonfire all the evening, and then, it seems when you've gone home with them—(*she turns to Hortensia*) the fire's dead out.

Hortensia. What is this new caprice of Tiger's, making her act with us? Of course, he's given a part to his valet as well, but I hope that once the play's over, he'll send her back to the kitchen.

Countess. Let me disillusion you once again. From what I know of Tiger, providing she has had a little success in the play—(*she crosses below the settee to* l, *picks up the Count's wig from the chair and puts it on the table down* l) he'll dance with her the entire evening. (*She stubs out her cigarette in the ashtray on the table down* l)

Hortensia. That would be most disagreeable. Until now, your house was one of the very rare places where one could be sure of meeting only one's friends.

Countess. I quite agree. Tiger refuses to meet his broker socially, but if he has decided that the goddaughter of my family solicitor can be received, received she will be.

Hortensia. It's grotesque! Isn't she some sort of nursemaid here?

Countess (*crossing to the settee*) If these children were our own, I doubt if Tiger would have dared. She is here to supervise the orphans left us in his aunt's will. (*She sits* l *of Hortensia on the settee*) All twelve

of them. Tiger has a genius for taking advantage of nuances. Besides
—I'd rather not hide it from you—I believe he was dying to have
her.

HORTENSIA. There is a certain bitterness in your remarks,
Eliane.

COUNTESS. Far be it from me to stoop to bitterness—or to spite.
Your liaison with Tiger is entirely agreeable to me. Since we are
both at liberty to do as we please, it pleases me to admit that you're
exactly the right person for him.

HORTENSIA (*rising and crossing to the mirror*) At all events, I give
you my word he won't dance the night through with her. (*She looks
in the mirror*)

COUNTESS. But no scenes! That would be the best way of making
up his mind for him.

HORTENSIA (*turning*) Thank you for your good advice, Eliane, but
I know Tiger fairly well myself.

COUNTESS (*rising*) Your dress is utterly delightful.

HORTSENSIA. Yours suits you to perfection.

COUNTESS (*crossing to Hortensia*) I can't tell you how grateful I
am to you for being beautiful. I should have been horribly mortified
if Tiger had taken up with a mere nobody. (*She looks at Hortensia's
dress*) How amusingly Jacquot has cut the skirt. He really is a genius.
(*She crosses to* RC)

HORTENSIA. Leonor still makes your clothes, doesn't she? Will
she be there?

COUNTESS. Who?

HORTENSIA (*a little spitefully*) Leonor. Of course she's coming.
That woman goes everywhere—(*she moves to* L *of the settee*) even to
Tiger's parties.

COUNTESS. Particularly to Tiger's parties.

HORTENSIA. Why particularly? Everyone knows that Leonor,
who began as a milliner's apprentice, has had a tremendous social
success. He's merely swimming with the tide.

COUNTESS. Tiger never swims with a tide he hasn't created himself. We must do him that justice. (*She moves up* R *of the settee*) He
feels sure enough of himself to ennoble whom he pleases. He invites
her into his house because he wants her, and because she said "no"
to him four years ago.

HORTENSIA. How sweet of you to tell me.

COUNTESS. I'm telling you because it's all old history. But to have
resisted Tiger—which is a pretty rare distinction, my dear—is quite
enough to get one received everywhere.

HORTENSIA (*moving* L) Eliane, you're wasting your barbs. Tiger
or anybody else, I am quite determined never to suffer.

COUNTESS. That's precisely why I believe he is so very attached
to you. (*She crosses to Hortensia*) And so am I. (*She kisses Hortensia*)

(*The* FOOTMAN *enters down* R *and stands to one side*)

Dear little Hortensia! After all, one has so few friends.

(HERO *enters down* R *and crosses to* RC. *He is carrying his wig*)

(*She crosses to Hero*) Ah! Hero! My little Hero! I love you very much.

(*The* FOOTMAN *exits down* R)

HERO. You took the words out of my mouth, Eliane.

(HORTENSIA *moves up* L)

(*He moves to the armchair* RC) Do we rehearse? Tiger is a tyrant, making us put on our costumes five days before the performance. I don't know how to move in mine.

COUNTESS. That's exactly why he wants us to get used to them.

(HORTENSIA *sits on the chair* L)

He says the reason why masked balls take so long to warm up is because everyone is wondering if his trousers are going to fall down.

HERO. There's nothing wrong with my trousers—it's my waistcoat that's too tight. All the same, he did say we could dispense with our wigs.

COUNTESS. Yes. (*She sits on the settee, at the left end of it*) It's the tyrant's latest whim.

HERO. Pity. It was the part I liked best. My hair is beginning to go.

COUNTESS. You're thirty-seven, Hero.

HERO. I'll be bald at forty. (*He moves up* C, *looking for somewhere to put his wig*) My doctor told me I spend too much time making love. I had a terrible quarrel with him. (*He throws his wig beneath the vine up* L)

HORTENSIA. Because he dared to tell you that?

HERO (*moving up* RC) No. Everyone in Paris knows I'm the original Squire of Dames. He was the one who started the quarrel. He has a beard like a prophet, and as much hair as Absolom. When he told me love makes a man bald, I couldn't help laughing in his face. "Doctor," I said, "I have the impression *you* don't get much fun out of life." He took it very badly.

COUNTESS. You ought to get married, Hero.

HERO (*moving to the armchair* RC) If you can't find me a woman who will make me forget all the others, it would only mean one woman more to satisfy. (*He sits in the armchair*) My strength wouldn't be up to it. And if you could make me fall in love, do you know of any breed of woman who quenches the thirst?

COUNTESS (*rising, moving along and sitting on the right end of the settee*) Hero, you play the cynic, and you're the most sentimental soul in the world. One has only to look at you.

HERO. Your love of paradox leads you astray, Eliane. This deep appealing look in my eyes is nothing but the yearnings of the drunkard. Of course I'm sentimental; but I like causing pain.

COUNTESS. I've never heard anyone really wicked admit that.

HERO. I'm not wicked. I like breaking things. It's a taste small boys lose as they grow up. I have never lost it.

HORTENSIA (*rising, crossing and standing behind Hero*) When will you make me suffer, Hero? I'm getting impatient.

HERO. Whenever you please, my dear. But it wouldn't amuse either of us. We're too alike. (*He takes Hortensia's hand without looking at her*)

(VILLEBOSSE *enters down* L. *He is to play the part of Harlequin and is costumed accordingly.* HERO *and* HORTENSIA *laugh at him*)

VILLEBOSSE. Have you heard the news?

HERO. Undoubtedly. We always hear everything before you do.

VILLEBOSSE. Apparently we're to appear without wigs. We'll all look ridiculous!

HERO (*rising*) I doubt if the wig could have saved you, Villebosse. (*He moves to the drinks on the table up* C) May I help myself, Eliane? (*He picks up a decanter and a glass*)

(HORTENSIA *moves up* R *and puts her script on the urn*)

COUNTESS. Oh, Hero! We're going to rehearse.

(HORTENSIA *goes out up* R *on to the terrace where she strolls from* R *to* L)

HERO (*moving behind the settee; decanter and glass in hand*) My talent lies at the bottom of a glass, Eliane—you know that perfectly well. (*He leans over the back of the settee and kisses her*)

(*The* COUNTESS *laughs*)

Unfortunately, I don't remember which one. (*He returns to the table up* C, *pours himself a drink, replaces the decanter then sits on the chair up* R) That's why I have to empty so many.

VILLEBOSSE (*removing his hat and crossing to the Countess*) My dear— (*he sits* L *of the Countess on the settee*) that man exasperates me. I will not have him paying his attentions to you.

COUNTESS. You bore me, Villebosse. I didn't take a lover just to listen to reproaches my husband never makes.

VILLEBOSSE. Tiger is a cynic and he doesn't love you. I do. I don't want to precipitate a scandal under your roof, but if that miserable sot allows himself to go too far, I'll slap his face without the least compunction.

COUNTESS. Hero is quite capable of slapping you back and refusing your challenge.

VILLEBOSSE. I'd publish it everywhere. He wouldn't dare show his face. He'd die of shame.

COUNTESS (*rising and crossing down* L) I don't feel that shame is likely to be the death of Hero. He swallowed shame a long time ago —along with everything else.

VILLEBOSSE (*with a glance at Hero*) You despise him, at least?

COUNTESS. I don't know.

VILLEBOSSE (*rising and crossing to the Countess*) For heaven's sake, Eliane. Tell me immediately that you despise him. If you don't, I'll pack my bags and I won't appear in the play.

COUNTESS. If you play such an unkind trick on Tiger, Villebosse, I'll never set eyes on you again.

VILLEBOSSE (*moving* LC *and turning to her*) Tiger's futilities are the least of my worries. Let him replace me as best he can. (*He moves to the Countess and kneels to her*) I love you, Eliane. I am your lover. Surely that counts for something?

COUNTESS. I'm beginning to find it counts prodigiously. You have succeeded in the paradox of making infidelity far more boring than virtue.

VILLEBOSSE (*rising*) Very well. I shall pretend not to know my part. I will ruin his production. (*He crosses and sits on the chair down* R) I'm tired of being the only one to suffer.

HERO (*rising; glass in hand*) What's Villebosse talking about?

COUNTESS. He says he's suffering.

(HORTENSIA *comes in* L *from the terrace*)

HERO. How interesting. Hortensia, my little heart of stone, come and look at this gracious natural phenomenon. (*He moves down* R *and stands behind Villebosse*)

(HORTENSIA *crosses and stands with Hero*)

A man suffering for love. We should never miss a chance of extending our knowledge.

VILLEBOSSE (*rising and turning his back*) Sir, I refuse to speak to you.

(*The* COUNTESS *makes a gesture to silence Villebosse, then sits on the chair down* L. VILLEBOSSE *resumes his seat.*
The FOOTMAN *enters down* L *and stands above the open door.* HORTENSIA *collects her script from the urn then stands* R *of the settee.* HERO *stands above the armchair* RC.
The COUNT *enters down* L, *holding* LUCILE *by the hand, and leads her down* C.
DAMIENS *follows them on, closes the door and stands near it*)

COUNT. I have valiantly rescued Silvia from the twelve monsters. (*He sucks his finger*) One tried to claw me. I bleed. Now, my children, we can begin. We're all here.

(*There is a pause during which the* FOOTMAN *crosses to the settee, moves it, sets it below the table up* C *and stands behind it. At the same time the* COUNT *moves up* L *and collects his prompt script.* LUCILE *moves up* L)

(*He moves down* C, *displaying his script*) *The Double Inconstancy* is a ruthless play. I must beg you not to forget it. Silvia and Harlequin are really in love. The Princes desires Silvia—perhaps he loves her, too? Why should princes always be refused the right to love as deeply, as simply, as Harlequin? The whole court, that is, the rest of you, will conspire to destroy the loves of Harlequin and Silvia, and so to arrange matters that Silvia shall fall in love with the Prince; Harlequin will love Flaminia, and they will each forget their first love. In short, it is the story of an elegant and sophisticated crime. (*He tosses his script on to the settee*) Villebosse——

(VILLEBOSSE *rises and crosses slowly to* L *of the sofa*)

—Harlequin is tender and good, but easy-going, greedy and simple. Flaminia and her sister are so beautiful, they smell so delicious! Never forget that, even when he rejects them and thinks tenderly of Silvia, he is still conscious of them in his nostrils. The good smell of silk on a scented skin—what a snare for the poor young lad.

(HERO *laughs.* DAMIENS *reacts to the laugh, moves to the chair up* L *and sits*)

Flaminia and Lisette—(*he crosses to Hortensia, takes her hand and leads her to the Countess down* L) her sister, hard, frivolous, flirtatious, playful; the country boy must smell good, too, to those fine, corrupted ladies. They play with him, show their claws, retract them—desire grows like curiosity—and besides, they are serving their Prince; the iron law of this little world. (*He moves* C) They are creatures of another race, they are well aware of it: and Harlequin is like a dear little dog with an amusing bark and a warm tongue. They let themselves be licked by the little dog, just below the loop of their pearls. It's a new sort of game and hurts nobody. I rather suspect that they have kept their real lovers in reserve. Eliane and Hortensia—I fancy it would be naïve of me to try and give you directions. You will do the whole thing beautifully. Silvia. (*He turns to Lucile*)

(LUCILE *moves down* LC)

What shall I say of Silvia? She's not romantic, she is tender; she isn't simple, she is good; she isn't hard, she is straightforward. She is dazzled neither by the fine ladies of the Court nor by the Prince. She is a clear and limpid being. In this luxurious universe, sneering under its silks, its precious stones, its plumes, she stands alone, bright and naked under her cotton frock: erect and silent, she watches them all as they whirl and plot around her. Suddenly, everything which has been made for the Prince's strength and pleasure falls to pieces in his hands—worthless. Silvia is a small, inaccessible being who stands watching him, a thousand leagues away, and troubles his heart. (*In spite of himself his voice changes slightly*) So something else besides pleasure exists in this world——

(HORTENSIA, *the* COUNTESS *and* HERO, *behind his glass, look at the Count in surprise*)

—and he did not know it. (*He breaks off*)

(*There is a slight pause*)

(*He turns slowly to Lucile. In a low voice*) But I have no need to explain the part to you, mademoiselle. You have only to be yourself.

The others, motionless, look at the Count as—

the CURTAIN *falls*

SCENE 2

SCENE—*The same. The following afternoon.*

When the CURTAIN *rises,* LUCILE *is seated in the armchair down* RC, *facing down* R. *The* COUNT *is standing up* RC.

COUNT. Yes, I know—I know it's wrong of me to talk to you like this, but I have reached middle-age and never yet had the strength to deny myself a pleasure.

(LUCILE *looks at him*)

Forgive me. I have pronounced the unforgiveable word. (*He shakes himself and moves to* R *of her*) I don't know what conspiracy of bigots and old maids has managed in two centuries to discredit the word "pleasure". It is one of the sweetest and noblest words in the language. I don't believe in God, but if I did, I am sure I should go to mass with pleasure. Good and evil, in the beginning, must have been what gave pleasure or what did not—as simple as that. Why shouldn't love be, above all, a pleasure of the heart? One has all the time in the world to pay the price for it. (*He crosses above Lucile to* L *of her and looks at her*) In any case, it's enthralling to be in love with a young girl who has lost her tongue. It lures one to soliloquy and meditation. One never talks to oneself enough. For years now, I haven't said a word to myself. I failed to appreciate myself: I am, in fact, a most agreeable companion. How much too quick we always are to judge by appearances. I find my nature both tender and profound.

LUCILE. You know quite well we're supposed to be rehearsing. The others must certainly be listening at the door.

COUNT. The dumb has spoken! How interesting it is when the dumb begin to speak. And—wonder of wonders—it isn't to ask me to be dumb, but merely to ask me to lower my voice.

LUCILE. If I had really wanted to stop you talking any time during the week I have been here, I should have done so. Girls have ways of doing it. Or I could have let you go on talking, and simply not listened. I am just afraid the others may be listening. That's all.

COUNT. Why will you never see me anywhere, except in here during rehearsals? What game are you playing, assuming I don't bore you?

B

LUCILE. No game at all, I promise. When I do fall in love with a man, the moment I'm sure of it, I shall do everything I can to give him pleasure—as you call it—without playing any game.

COUNT. I wonder what virtues or what guarantees you'll expect from that important person?

LUCILE. None. I shall belong to him, even if he's poor, even if he doesn't know where to sleep at night: even if he has a wife and children, and can only spare one hour a week when we can meet in a café.

COUNT (*moving above Lucile to* R *of her; with a trace of temper*) Particularly if he's poor, of course—particularly if he doesn't know where he'll sleep the night. You're all the same—if you're not taken by force, then you always have to pity a man before you give yourself to him.

LUCILE (*gently*) Even if he is rich and happy. It's exactly the same thing.

COUNT. Very well! I am rich and happy and I want you to love me.

LUCILE. Little children also cry for the moon. It's my job to explain that they can't have it so easily. You believe I don't want to love you? You or anybody else? It must be so wonderful to give everything.

COUNT. Mustn't it? And it all fits in beautifully, because I am a beggar.

LUCILE. My poor Monsieur—one can only give to the rich.

COUNT. Explain yourself, if you please. I always came bottom in divinity—I could never make head or tail of the parables.

LUCILE. The man who loves me as I want to be loved, won't need to ask.

COUNT. How will you know he loves you? Because he tells you so, poor baby. (*He moves up* C)

LUCILE. No. Because he probably won't even think of telling me. And certainly not so amusingly as you do.

COUNT (*moving to* L *of her*) What will this paragon do? Talk about the moon? Sigh and groan? Throw himself on his knees?

LUCILE. He'll be shy—I don't suppose he'll say a word. He may even avoid my eyes. He will ask another girl to dance, but I shall know I'm the one he really loves.

COUNT (*after a slight pause*) The rules seem a trifle complicated. But I shall learn. I'm very good at all games. (*He crosses to* LC)

LUCILE. I'm afraid this one can't be taught.

COUNT. When I am in love, I want to be loved. (*He turns to her*) I want to shine—to dazzle. Cocks ruffle their feathers. It must be a natural reaction.

LUCILE. I shall want the man I love not to be able to find exactly the right word when he loves me—I hope he will be as startled as I. But please let's rehearse. We are gossiping and we'll never be ready. It would be terrible, wouldn't it, if we didn't know our parts?

COUNT (*crossing to her*) Very well.

(LUCILE *rises*)

Thank you for putting me so gently in my place. I'm an ass. As a boy, I was somewhat spoiled and I have many grave faults, it's true. Forget the whole thing and let's rehearse. You're quite right. (*He moves down* L)

(LUCILE *crosses above the armchair, stands* L *of it and faces* R. *They commence the rehearsal*)

"How's this, Silvia? You will not look . . ." (*He breaks off and crosses to Lucile*) One word more. During the week you've been here, I've been asking myself why I can think of nothing but you. I've told you as much—in my own way.

(LUCILE *moves a step* R)

You've made it clear that either the matter or the manner fails to please you. Good. I've been well brought up. I shan't chase you down the corridors, trying to put my arm round your waist. Neither shall I throw myself in the pond. Between those two extremes there is a golden mean: mere regret for the loss of a charming adventure, nothing more. You're an adorable child. Let us rehearse. As you say—(*he crosses down* L) the others may be listening. (*He gestures to Lucile to get into her place*)

(LUCILE *moves to* L *of the armchair, as before, and faces* R. *They recommence the rehearsal*)

"How's this, Silvia? You will not look at me? Each time that I accost you, you grow sad."

LUCILE (*turning to him and smiling*) You know, you're very sweet.

COUNT. Sweet?

LUCILE. You're still the little boy with his white gloves, his stick and his very first bowler hat who took his constitutional every morning in the Avenue du Bois.

COUNT. What? Who told you that? In the days of my first bowler, you were still puling in your cot, little girl.

LUCILE. That doesn't matter. I can just see you. It's difficult to grow up, isn't it? But, please—let's rehearse. (*She turns to face* R)

COUNT (*crossing above Lucile and sitting in the armchair*) It's most disconcerting. You look at me kindly for the first time, and for what? To drown me in your pity. No-one's ever played that trick on me before. Yes, I did wear a bowler. Yes, I did go for a stroll in the Avenue du Bois before lunch, every morning. I don't think I was so absurd. At any rate, the girls of your age—in those days—didn't think so.

LUCILE. You mustn't lose your temper. It's rather good to have remained a little boy.

COUNT (*rising and crossing above Lucile to* L *of her*) But I'm not a little boy. I've been through the war. I had a cannon—a real cannon. They gave me a medal, as they do to little boys, of course, but I never wear it. For fifteen years I have given the most successful balls in Paris—grown-up ones, too. At one time I was a diplomat, and if I'd stuck it out, I might be representing France somewhere or other at this very moment. I don't know what else to tell you. I'm a man like other men—rather more brilliant than other men, or so I'm told. I'm tired of listening to your tiny fluting like a great subjugated snake. Let us rehearse. (*He moves down* L)

LUCILE (*moving to him*) You mustn't listen to the gossip of girls. You'll be dreadfully misled.

COUNT. My dearest child . . .

LUCILE. Treat me as I deserve. I shan't take offence.

COUNT (*still in a temper*) But I'm not listening to you! I am merely astonished. Come on, come on—rehearse. I am making a fool of myself, and *you're* playing a game, whatever you say, and playing it a good deal more wittily than I am. I know how to be a good loser —that, also, is part of my excellent upbringing. But don't go round boasting about it. That's all I ask.

LUCILE. Boasting? To whom?

COUNT. How should I know? To your godfather—your girl-friends . . .

LUCILE. I never speak to my godfather. You must have noticed that there's not much love lost between us. And I have no girl-friends.

COUNT. Good. To your twelve little orphans, perhaps.

LUCILE. Oh, I shall tell them, of course. I have to tell them so many magical stories. But I shall change the context. This will all take place in the Middle Ages. Besides, they never understand any-thing—they're asleep long before the end.

COUNT. Splendid. Let us rehearse.

(LUCILE *moves to her place at the armchair and they proceed to rehearse*)

"How's this, Silvia? You will not look at me? Each time that I accost you, you grow sad. It grieves me to suppose myself importu-nate." (*He crosses to Lucile*)

LUCILE. "Importunate? I was speaking of you only just now."

COUNT. "Speaking of me? And what, fair Silvia, did you say?"

LUCILE (*crossing below the Count to* L) "Oh, I said many things. I said that you do not yet know what I am thinking."

COUNT (*moving to* R *of Lucile*) "I know you are resolved to refuse me your heart, and thereby I know your thoughts."

LUCILE (*with her back to him*) "You are not so clever as you think. Do not boast so much."

COUNT. That's it, of course! You lied to me—you do love some-one. Some little man you write a four-page letter to every night before you go to sleep.

LUCILE. I don't think you are keeping to the lines.

COUNT. I must ask you one question. The others are coming. Give me a straight answer.

LUCILE (*turning and looking at him; gravely*) No. I am not in love.
I have never been in love with anyone.

(*The* COUNTESS, DAMIENS, HORTENSIA, VILLEBOSSE *and the*
FOOTMAN *enter up* R. DAMIENS *goes down* R. HORTENSIA *crosses to* L
of the table up C. VILLEBOSSE *stands* R. *The* FOOTMAN *closes the door
then stands* R *of the settee*)

COUNTESS (*crossing to* L *of the armchair*) Well—how goes the last
scene?
COUNT (*turning to the Countess*) Extremely well. We think we're
both very talented.
COUNTESS. We others, who are not so gifted, had better rehearse,
too.
COUNT. Would you like to go through the whole play? Monsieur
Damiens says he's still very shaky.
COUNTESS. Monsieur Damiens is used to speaking in public.

(HERO, *glass in hand, enters down* L. *He looks at the Count, Lucile and
the Countess, then moves up* LC)

Besides, we haven't time to go through the whole play before dinner.
We can do that later.
COUNT. In that case, let's start with the beginning of Act Two.

(*The* FOOTMAN *moves the armchair to* LC *then stands behind the settee.*
DAMIENS *moves* RC. *The* COUNTESS *moves and stands below Damiens*)

We can cut Silvia's long speeches. (*He moves to Hortensia and leads her
to* R *of the armchair*) My dear Hortensia, we are doing this for your
benefit. I think you are a little too acid in your scene with Silvia.
You are underlining too much. Be charming, as I know you can.
You have to deceive the girl, remember.
HORTENSIA (*immediately taking offence*) If you don't think I'm
up to the part, my dear Tiger, you can replace me.

(*The* COUNTESS *signs to Damiens to move the chair* R *to down* R *of
the settee.* DAMIENS *moves the chair and the* COUNTESS *sits on it.* DAMIENS
stands behind her)

COUNT. Hortensia, it fits you like a glove. I am merely asking
for a trifle more subtlety. (*He crosses to* R) Actors are the most impossible people.

(HORTENSIA *sits in the armchair*)

Don't make the mistake of believing it's enough to reproduce the
realities of life. (*He collects his script from the sofa*)

(HERO *moves to the table up* C, *refills his glass then stands up* LC. *The*
FOOTMAN *moves the settee to* R)

The object of art is to give life a shape, and to do it by every con-
ceivable artifice. Beginning—Act Two. Silvia speaks. (*He hands his
script to the Footman, beckons to Lucile then crosses to* L)

(*The* FOOTMAN *crosses and sits on the chair down* L. LUCILE *crosses to* C)

LUCILE (*to Hortensia*) "Yes, I believe you. You seem to wish me well, but you may perceive that I am suffering as cruelly as you. I regard the others as my enemies. (*She crosses to* RC) But where is Harlequin?"

HORTENSIA. "He will come soon—he is still dining."

(HERO *glances at* VILLEBOSSE *sulking in his corner*)

HERO (*into his glass*) Wrong! He's not dining, he's suffering. If he seems to be dining, it's because he's chewing the cud of his spite.

VILLEBOSSE (*with a step towards Hero*) Monsieur, I have already told you I'm not speaking to you. My patience has its limits, you know.

COUNT. Hero—do be serious for once.

HERO. Impossible, dear boy—I'm not drunk yet. I'll be serious later.

(*The* COUNT *signs to Lucile to continue*)

LUCILE (*crossing to* R *of Hortensia*) "There is something frightening about this country. Never have I seen women so well-bred, or men so courteous. Their manners are delightful, so many curtsies, so many compliments, so many marks of friendship."

(VILLEBOSSE *crosses and sits on the chair up* L)

"You would say they were the best people on earth, that they were full of goodness and sensibility. What an error of judgement." (*To the Count*) Shall I cut?

(*The* COUNT *crosses above the armchair to* L *of Lucile and looks at her script*)

COUNT. Yes, yes. Cut. You say all that very well. (*He indicates a place in the script*) "To be worthless . . ."

LUCILE. "To be worthless, to deceive their neighbours, to cheat, to lie. That's what they want, the ladies and gentlemen of this accursed place. What can these people be? Where do they come from? Of what clay are they made?"

(HERO *crosses and stands up* RC. *The* COUNT *turns to Hortensia and looks at her*)

HORTENSIA. "The same clay as other men, my dear Silvia, which shouldn't surprise you. They believe the Prince's marriage will make for your happiness." (*She gives the Count a false smile*)

LUCILE (*moving down* R) "But am I not required to be faithful? Is it not my duty as an honest girl? And when one fails in one's duty, can one be happy? Besides, is not this fidelity my touchstone?" (*To the Count*) Shall I cut?

COUNT. No. I'm enjoying it too much. Go on.

LUCILE. "And none of them has the courage to say: there—play an evil trick which will bring you nothing but harm—throw away your joy and your integrity. And because I refuse, they call me obstinate."

HORTENSIA. "What do you expect? These people think in their own fashion, desire nought but happiness for their Prince."

COUNT. Good, Hortensia! (*He moves down* R)

LUCILE (*moving to Hortensia and kneeling to her*) "But why does the Prince not take some girl who would give herself willingly? How strange a fancy to want the very one who does not want him." (*She looks towards the Count*) "What pleasure can he find in that?" (*She giggles*)

COUNTESS (*to the Count*) Tell her the Prince isn't on stage, Tiger. She should be looking at Hortensia.

(*The* COUNT, *watching Lucile, circles the settee and stands down* R *of it*)

LUCILE (*rising*) "Everything he does is wrong. All these concerts, these plays, these jewels he sends me. It's costing him a fortune. Ask me what he seeks to gain." (*She crosses to the settee*) "If he loaded me with the entire contents of a jeweller's shop, it wouldn't please me half so much as the skein of wool that Harlequin gave me." (*She sits on the settee*)

HORTENSIA (*rising and moving* C) "No doubt of it. That is true love. I, too, have loved like that. And I, too, have preferred a skein of wool . . ." (*To the Count*) Does she mean it when she says that? I feel I sound insincere. Has she ever really been in love? Did she really once prefer a little skein of wool to all the Prince's jewels?

COUNT. What about you, Hortsensia dear?

(HERO *crosses above the others to* L)

HORTENSIA. Tiger, it's nothing to do with me. If this is a game you're playing, it isn't funny.

COUNT. Forgive me. When I cast the play, I knew quite well what I was doing. (*He crosses to* R *of Hortensia*) You said that line perfectly.

HORTENSIA. I tried to make it sincere.

COUNT. Since you've never preferred a small skein of wool to your own pleasures, in saying the line "sincerely", you sounded abominably false. It was perfect. Just what I wanted. (*He crosses below Hortensia and stands above the chair* L) Go on.

HORTENSIA. You're treating us all like puppets. You'll exhaust our patience soon.

COUNT. All directors of real genius do that. You can be grateful I don't go in for tearing up the script and screaming. Go on, Silvia —go on. (*He looks at the prompt script*) "Ah well! Let him try to forget me, then."

LUCILE (*rising and moving to Hortensia*) "Ah, well! Let him try to forget me, then, send me away, turn to another."

(*The* COUNT *moves down* L, *looking at Hortensia*)

"There are many here who have their lovers as I do, but that doesn't stop them loving other people. I'm aware that it means nothing to them. But for me, it's impossible."

HORTENSIA. "My dear child, have we anyone here to match you in beauty and virtue?" (*She smiles forcedly, then turns and looks at the Count*)

COUNT. Excellent—the poison beneath the smile. You must have worked all night to get that so exactly, Hortensia.

(HORTENSIA *crosses and sits on the settee at the downstage end of it*)

LUCILE (*turning to Hortensia*) "Oh, but you have. There are many fairer than I and even were they half as pretty, they know better than I how to make the most of their beauty." (*She looks at the Countess*) "I have seen ugly people here who make such beautiful faces that one is quite deceived."

COUNTESS. It's Flaminia you're looking at, my child. I'm not on stage yet—my entrance comes later.

HORTENSIA. "Yes, but your beauty is natural, and that is so charming."

LUCILE. "I am nothing beside the others. They always seem happy. Their eyes caress the whole world. They must be far more attractive than a humble girl like me who dares not raise her eyes, and blushes when someone finds her beautiful."

COUNTESS. I feel she ought to say that line more modestly. Don't you think so, Tiger? She looks as though she's attacking in her turn.

COUNT (*moving to L of Lucile*) But of course she is attacking—she attacks. Everybody's beginning to want her to attack.

COUNTESS. Besides, Mademoiselle is charming—we all think so. I think you were quite right to give her the part. All the same— I can say it in front of her, because I know she's very intelligent— she hasn't quite enough glamour to justify the confidence in her own beauty which shows in the text. She should say the line more simply.

COUNT (*moving up LC*) I don't agree with you. I think she says it perfectly. Go on, Hortensia.

HORTENSIA. "But that's precisely what has moved the Prince. It's what he admires. Such innocence, such beauty unadorned, such natural grace. And if you'll take a hint from me, don't praise these ladies so generously, because they will not return the compliment."

LUCILE. "What do they say about me?"

HORTENSIA. "Impertinences. They make fun of you, tease the Prince, ask him for news of his rustic beauty. 'Was there ever so commonplace a countenance, so gawky a manner?' said those jealous ones the other day. Thereupon one dispraised your eyes, another your lips. Even the men had some fault to find with you. Oh, it put me in such a fury."

LUCILE. "Lud! What wretches they must be, denying their real feelings to please all those idiots." (*She crosses above the sofa to* R *of it*)

COUNT. Isn't she amusing? (*To Hero*) Don't you think she's amusing when she says that? (*He moves down* L) I adore this little character.

HORTENSIA. "It takes little to please them." Don't interrupt all the time, Tiger—it's maddening. (*She repeats*) "It takes little to please them."

LUCILE. "How I hate such women. But since their opinion of me is so low, why does the Prince love me, and abandon them?"

HORTENSIA. "Oh, they're convinced he will not love you long; that it's merely a passing fancy, that he'll leave you all the sooner." (*She smiles forcedly*)

COUNT (*crossing to Hortensia*) Heavens, how well you said that, Hortensia. You've got it, my dear, you've only to carry on like that. Let's cut the rest and go on to my entrance with Eliane. That's very important.

(*The* FOOTMAN *rises and draws the armchair to* L. *The* COUNT *moves down* L. *The* COUNTESS *rises and crosses to* R *of the Count.* HORTENSIA *rises and moves behind the settee.* LUCILE *moves to the settee and sits on it at the upstage end.* DAMIENS *sets a chair down* R, *then moves up* RC. *The* FOOTMAN *returns to his seat at the table* L)

Come along, Eliane—our cue.

(*The* COUNTESS *crosses, takes the* COUNT'S *hand and they cross to* C. LUCILE *rises, leaves her script on the settee and moves down* RC)

LUCILE. "What, is it you, sir? Were you then aware of my presence here?"

COUNT (*bowing*) Yes, Mademoiselle. But you commanded me never to see you again and I should never have dared to show myself without madame, who desired me to accompany her, having obtained from the Prince the honour of making you a curtsy."

LUCILE (*with a step towards the Count*) "I am not angry at seeing you, but you find me in low spirits. As for this lady, I thank her for her kindness in wishing to make me a curtsy. She may do so if she pleases."

(*The* COUNTESS *curtsies to Lucile*)

"I shall do the same, to the best of my ability. She will pardon me if I do it clumsily." (*She curtsies to the Countess*)

COUNTESS. "With all my heart. I do not ask you to perform the impossible."

(LUCILE *moves down* R, *looking at the Countess over her shoulder*)

LUCILE. "To perform the impossible! What a thing to say!"
COUNTESS. "Child, how old are you?"
LUCILE (*looking at the Countess*) "Mother, I have forgotten."
HORTENSIA (*to Lucile*) "Bravo!"

COUNTESS (*looking at the Count*) "She is angry, I think."

COUNT. "Madame, what is the meaning of this? Under pretext of paying your respects to Silvia, you insult her?"

COUNTESS. "Such was not my intention. But I was curious to see this child, who inspires such a love, who arouses so fierce a passion and to find out for myself what makes her so desirable. They say she's naïve—there's a rustic charm about that which ought to be amusing. Ask her to give us a taste of her simplicity. Let us judge of her wit."

LUCILE (*sitting on the settee*) "Oh, dear me, no, madame! It isn't worth the trouble. My wit is not so sprightly as yours."

HORTENSIA. "Ah! Ah! You asked for simplicity—and here it is."

COUNT (*pointing to the door* L; *to the Countess*) "Leave us, madame."

COUNTESS. "I shall be out of patience soon. If she doesn't go, I shall go myself at once."

COUNT. "You will answer to me for your actions."

COUNTESS. "Farewell! Such a choice revenges me enough upon the chooser."

COUNT (*turning to the Countess*) Perfect. Scene Three.

COUNTESS (*carrying on; almost on the same tone*) Enough. I'm tired and I'd like to have a word with you, Tiger. Will you please come up to my room.

HORTENSIA. Good idea—let's stop for a while. Tiger finds it all tremendously amusing—I don't think we enjoy it so much. We all need a breathing space, my dear. (*She moves to the door up* R)

(DAMIENS *opens the door for Hortensia.*
HORTENSIA *exits up* R. DAMIENS *closes the door and stands up* RC.
The FOOTMAN *rises, puts the prompt script on his chair then exits down* L *leaving the door open*)

COUNT (*looking at his watch*) Very well—we'll stop. The rehearsal will start again in fifteen minutes.

(*The* COUNTESS *crosses to the door down* R *and opens it*)

(*He moves to Hero*) My dear Hero, women don't understand the theatre. It's no fun for them to be anything but themselves.

(*The* COUNTESS *pauses by the door, waiting for the Count*)

HERO. They should take to drink—that makes all games amusing. You, too, Villebosse.

VILLEBOSSE (*rising*) One day, sir, I'll suggest a game you'll find far less amusing.

(VILLEBOSSE *exits down* L.
The FOOTMAN *is seen crossing the terrace from* L *to* R)

COUNTESS. Well, Tiger? Are you coming?

(*The* COUNT *crosses to the* COUNTESS *and they exit down* R, *leaving the door open. As the Count exits,* LUCILE *looks after him, picks up her script and rises)*

HERO (*moving* LC; *glass in hand*) Mademoiselle——

(LUCILE *turns to Hero*)

—your performance is quite exquisite. That's the opinion of a drunk: I drank in every word. I was so absorbed the whole time, I forgot to drink anything else. Tomorrow I shall write and tell my doctor and doubtless he will send you a note of thanks. I'm going to get out of this rig. My waistcoat is too tight. (*He moves to Lucile*) Although I've never touched a drop of water in my life, they tell me I have gallons of it in my belly. Life is full of such curious contradictions. (*He moves close to her*) You didn't know that yet, did you, dear heart?

(LUCILE *imperceptibly draws away*)

You draw away? I smell, perhaps? I smell of alcohol. What else do you expect me to smell of? But it isn't such a bad smell. They pickle the livers of famous drunkards in alcohol to frighten good little boys. Do I frighten you?

LUCILE. No.

HERO. That's because you can't see my liver. Apparently it's an appalling efflorescence. A virgin forest of many-coloured blossoms. I see you don't like flowers. That's all right. No doubt I disgust you?

(LUCILE *does not reply*)

(*He is very close to her, glass in hand. He smiles maliciously*) That's all right, too. I ought to disgust you a little. It's in my part. Not my part in the Marivaux—the one I play in real life. (*He crosses above the settee to the door down* R. *To Damiens*) I think your goddaughter is quite charming, Monsieur Damiens, but if, instead of being called Hero de . . . I won't bother you with my name, it is much too long— I were simple Monsieur Damiens, I swear to you I'd take her out of here. (*He smiles*) Word of a drunkard.

(HERO *exits down* R. LUCILE *moves towards the door down* L)

DAMIENS (*intercepting Lucile*) I must talk to you, Lucile. (*He crosses to the door down* R *and closes it*)

LUCILE (*reserved*) I'm listening.

DAMIENS (*moving behind the settee*) You are young. You do not know much of the world, nor of life. When your poor mother died, you wished to work in order to be independent, and that showed the right spirit. All the same, you know, you weren't obliged . . .

LUCILE (*turning to face him*) Not obliged? Mother lived on her widow's pension. When she died, I was left with a Rennaissance dining-table, three Regency chairs we always thought were real but which turned out to be fakes, my gramophone and an old cat. What else could I do?

DAMIENS. I was there.

LUCILE. You are my godfather, of course. It was very kind of you to want to help—(*she turns away*) but I did not want to owe you anything.

DAMIENS (*gently*) Why not, Lucile?

LUCILE (*moving down* L) You know why not.

DAMIENS (*moving in front of the settee*) My proposal seemed monstrous to you at first sight. God knows what a girl of eighteen dreams of. (*He tosses his script on to the settee and crosses towards Lucile*) That's why I left you alone. I wanted life and hard work to teach you a little wisdom, to show you what they have to offer in reality. I know these two years have been very hard for you.

LUCILE. Have I complained?

DAMIENS. Never, no, for you have a great deal of pride. But do you think I liked watching you struggling at the end of the month, with the little hat you had retrimmed a hundred times? With your gloves in holes and your worn-out stockings? (*He looks her up and down*) You are pretty, and I know that at your age a girl wants pretty clothes. I should have liked to have made things easier for you.

LUCILE (*with her back to him*) I should have liked it, too—I'm no heroine. But not from you.

DAMIENS. You are alone in the world. (*He moves, stands behind Lucile and puts his hands on her arms*) I had the right—I should have thought. The duty, even . . .

(LUCILE *makes a quick move below the armchair and turns to face Damiens*)

LUCILE. Please don't begin this conversation all over again. You know it distresses me. When I was a child you brought me dolls and sewing baskets, and then you found this position for me. You have more than done your duty. Now I can manage alone.

DAMIENS. Why won't you let me give you the security you need?

LUCILE. At my age, one doesn't ask for security.

DAMIENS. I don't mean just material security. I mean—a sincere affection. Care. Protection.

LUCILE (*with a step towards Damiens and looking squarely at him*) Whom will you protect me against, if I accept your proposition? Against other men who might propose the same thing as yourself?

DAMIENS (*a little more sharply*) Against less worthy men, without the love and respect I have for you. Men who might think only of an evening's enjoyment.

LUCILE (*crossing to the downstage end of the settee*) Haven't you learnt that I know how to protect myself?

DAMIENS. Perhaps against me: I was honest enough to tell you what I was offering. (*He moves* C) But against another, younger and more attractive . . .

LUCILE. If he were younger and more attractive, it would at any rate be less depressing, even if it didn't last so long. (*She throws her script on to the settee and crosses below it to* R *of it*) Particularly if it didn't last so long. And at least the enjoyment might be mutual.

DAMIENS. I hate to hear you speak so cynically. I wish now that I'd never brought you into this house. (*He moves up* C)

LUCILE. Why? Because they put me into costume and made me do two jobs for the price of one? In my situation I know one has to accept certain things. The matron of the children's home where I first went to work, taught me I had to sing for my supper. I know my place. And if that's what you hoped life would teach me, the lesson has been learned.

DAMIENS (*moving to* L *of the settee*) My dear child, the Count wants you, and he won't stop till he gets what he wants. Everyone here has seen what he's up to. You must have noticed it yourself during that rehearsal? (*He moves to Lucile and takes her by the arm*) The Countess is a clever woman: she overlooks his mistresses as he, for his part, overlooks her lovers, provided the game is played within their own world, with cards she recognizes. She will never let him pay court to you. She'll heap you with humiliations. Send you packing.

LUCILE (*moving away a step to* R) Is that what you're so afraid of? That I might lose my job? Don't worry, I should go to another children's home, that's all. All children are alike.

(DAMIENS *moves to* L *of the settee*)

They all make the same little messes at the same inconvenient moments. There is one thing you don't know—how rich one can be, when one has nothing to lose. (*She moves to* R *of the settee*)

DAMIENS (*facing her*) You couldn't be that man's mistress!

LUCILE. Don't be afraid—I shan't. But for quite different reasons, which only concern me.

DAMIENS. He's making a fool of you: he's a libertine—a . . .

(*The* COUNT *enters abruptly down* R. *He is a little pale*)

COUNT (*crossing above the settee to the armchair* L) Forgive me, Monsieur Damiens, I must carry off your goddaughter again.

(LUCILE *moves up* RC)

I have a scene with her to put right before this evening's rehearsal. Will you excuse me?

DAMIENS (*stiffly*) I place her in your care, sir. I have just been putting her on guard against the temptations of a world and a life which are not her own. (*He picks up his script and turns to the Count*) I do not wish her to forget that she is here to earn her living and to look after the children.

COUNT. My dear Damiens! On the contrary I shall do my best to try and make her forget it. Mademoiselle Lucile is my guest. If, in addition to the honour she has done us in agreeing to act—with far more talent than we—in this comedy of Marivaux, she is brave enough and kind enough to look after my aunt's little monsters—

instead of sleeping till midday like the other ladies in this château —that is yet another reason why we should be grateful to her. I hope to make that clear to everyone.

DAMIENS. If you will be good enough to undertake that task yourself, sir, then I shall leave you, completely reassured.

(DAMIENS *bows and exits down* R, *closing the door after him. The* COUNT *moves up* C. *As the door closes,* LUCILE *moves to the downstage end of the settee*)

COUNT (*moving to the settee*) No—don't say anything, Lucile. I owe you an apology. All my life, I've been surrounded by charming cads: I've grown so used to it that I've probably become one myself. (*He moves* C) Before the performance, there's nothing to be done; an entertainment is an entertainment, and this one has to be given. They will all make your life unbearable, but I know you're a brave girl. I have just had a conversation with my wife, and I, who thought I knew everything, have just discovered how far a woman of taste and intelligence can let herself go. For they have all realized that I love you, and that it isn't a caprice. So this is what I propose. Say nothing, please, until I have finished. It must be obvious to you that I can't agree to go on with my pleasant, trivial life of pleasure while you somewhere in this vast world, are busy blowing children's noses and cleaning up after them—children who aren't even your own. You're worth more than that—worth more than anything I can offer you.

(LUCILE *turns slightly away*)

I have very little money—you can rest easy on that score. I swallowed up my inheritance many moons ago, but by selling the few heirlooms that remain to me—(*he moves to her*) I can raise enough to send you abroad. You can go back to your studies—you'll be free— (*he crosses to* LC) and I shall hope with all my heart that within a few years, or a few months, you will find a lad of your own age worthy of you, who will help you to build a proper life. I shall never see you again. (*He pauses*)

(LUCILE *bows her head*)

I can see the talk of money embarrasses you, but unfortunately one can't avoid it. Money means nothing to free souls—it's a meaningless symbol. One mustn't be too middle-class about money. I merely ask you very humbly to share what I have left. You can leave the day after the performance. (*He pauses*) Of course this is the proposition of an egoist. An egoist who has never held you in his arms, not even once, and who is very unhappy. (*Very humbly*) Will you agree?

LUCILE (*turning and looking at him*) No. Of course not.

(*The* COUNT *looks at her, bewildered*)

(*Gently*) Now, I would rather stay.

(*The* Count *looks at her for a moment, hesitating, then crosses to her and suddenly takes her in his arms and kisses her*)

Count. My little girl.

Lucile (*nestling in his arms*) It's so wonderful! Is this what they call tenderness? I thought that only came much later on.

Count. So did I. We must have been very quick.

Lucile. We've done it properly. This is the right way.

(*They are in each other's arms*)

(*Suddenly*) I'm afraid.

Count. Of what?

Lucile. That I won't be able to please you for long. I'm not beautiful.

Count. You are.

Lucile. Not like Hortensia.

Count. No. Thank goodness.

Lucile. I'm not clever.

Count. Are you stupid enough to want me to agree?

Lucile. I can never think of anything funny to say at the right time.

Count. I should hope not. (*He takes her hands*)

Lucile. I'm poor. It's not the condition that's serious, it's the habit. I dress badly, and if I had any money for clothes, I might dress myself even worse. You have only to look at my hands to see that I'm no stranger to the washing-up—and even to the wash-tub —anyway, that I've had to work with my hands.

(*The* Count, *still holding her hands, moves away a step*)

What is there in me to attract you, once the novelty has worn off?

(*They sit together on the settee,* Lucile *at the downstage end*)

Count. Not being beautiful like the others, being awkward, being poor; not to have painted claws cluttered with flashy stones— (*he takes her hand*) but two little bare hands with short nails, hard-working hands. Hands of a real woman.

Lucile. If I thought it was just a fancy for beggar-maids which attracts you, I'd die of shame.

Count. It would be foolish of you not to understand, you who understand everything.

Lucile. Everyone will believe that's why I love you.

Count. Be sure they'll play that for all they're worth to drive us apart. But do you believe it? Do you?

Lucile. No.

Count. Neither do I. Don't be foolish. Well, if neither of us believes it, who is this "everyone" you're babbling about? Show me.

Lucile (*glancing at the door down* R) Why, there.

Count. Walk-ons, that's all. Small parts in this private play we're going to act together.

(*The* COUNTESS *enters up* R, *glances at the Count and Lucile and crosses to the table down* L.

HERO *enters up* R, *crosses to* L *of the table up* C *and helps himself to a drink.*

DAMIENS *enters down* R *and stands below the door.*

HORTENSIA *enters up* R *and moves to* R *of the settee.*

The FOOTMAN *enters up* R *and closes the door*)

(*He continues in a loud voice*) "Yes, Silvia, I have concealed my rank from you until this moment in order to awaken your love only by mine, nothing more. I could not bear to lose the joy it might bring me. Now you know who I am, you are at liberty to accept my hand and heart or to reject them both . . ." etc. etc. (*He rises, bows to the others and crosses to the Countess*) You're all very punctual, thank you. (*He crosses to* RC, *looking hard at Hortensia*) I hope you had a good rest. If you don't mind, before we go through the play again, we might turn our attention to an important item. Professional actors never forget to rehearse it before the first night. They spend all the time necessary on it, even if the play itself isn't quite perfect. I mean the curtain calls.

(*The* FOOTMAN *moves to the door down* R)

This is what I suggest and what seems to me most logical. (*He crosses to* C *and holds out his left hand to Lucile*)

(LUCILE *rises and crosses to the Count*)

(*He passes Lucile over to his left*) I give my hand to Lucile, with Eliane on my right.

(*The* COUNTESS *crosses to* R *of the Count and gestures to the Footman to move the settee. The* FOOTMAN *moves the settee up* RC *and stands behind it*)

Hortensia on Eliane's right, Hero and Villebosse on Lucile's left, then Damiens.

(HORTENSIA *moves to* R *of the Countess.* DAMIENS *crosses above the others to* L)

(*He moves down* L *and faces the others*) Where's Villebosse?

(VILLEBOSSE, *furious as usual, enters down* L)

VILLEBOSSE. They told me we were going to rehearse on the terrace. It's four o'clock. Do we rehearse or do we not?

COUNT. Just a second, Villebosse. For the moment, we're going to do something even more important in the theatre. Take our calls. (*He pushes Villebosse into place, then indicates to the others to bow*)

The others bow. HERO *crosses to* R *of Hortensia, winks at the Count and toasts him as—*

the CURTAIN *falls*

ACT II

SCENE—*The same. The afternoon of the following day.*

When the CURTAIN *rises, the settee is* LC *and the armchair is* RC. HORTENSIA *is seated in the armchair. The* COUNTESS *is pacing nervously from* R *to* L *and* L *to* R, *in silence.* VILLEBOSSE *enters down* L.

VILLEBOSSE (*standing above the settee*) Now, look here, do we rehearse or do we not?

COUNTESS. You're disturbing us, Villebosse.

VILLEBOSSE. What on earth has been going on since yesterday? We rehearse without any expression—or else give certain lines far too much, as if they were charged with overtones that quite escape me—everyone sniggers suddenly and nobody knows why: everyone insults everyone else: the little girl's in tears; Tiger blushes scarlet and leaves the rehearsal. Today we're starting an hour late. (*He sits on the settee,* C *of it*) We have to give a performance in three days' time and I have an enormous part. I won't be made to look ridiculous.

COUNTESS (*crossing and standing behind the downstage end of the settee*) Go away, Villebosse. I want to talk to Hortensia.

VILLEBOSSE. Eliane, I don't understand you, either. The way you treat me is utterly baffling. What on earth have I done?

COUNTESS. Nothing. Absolutely nothing. That's the whole point. Leave us alone.

VILLEBOSSE. But I'm suffering, Eliane.

COUNTESS. Then go and suffer in the garden. I want to talk to Hortensia. I'll call you back later.

VILLEBOSSE (*rising and moving up* C) I'll leave you, but I'm at the end of my patience. I'll wait on the terrace till you call. You owe me an explanation.

COUNTESS (*crossing to Villebosse*) You'll get it. We'll all get it. (*She kisses him*)

(VILLEBOSSE *smiles sweetly at the Countess then exits up* R)

(*She turns to Hortensia*) My dear Hortensia, I don't understand you. (*She moves to* R *of the settee*) For goodness' sake! He's courting this girl: he's mad about her—it's obvious to the meanest intelligence. And you do nothing, absolutely nothing.

HORTENSIA. I think he's revolting.

COUNTESS (*moving above the settee*) It's no use finding him revolting and not lifting a finger. Good God, if I were Tiger's mistress, I shouldn't allow myself to be made a fool of like this.

HORTENSIA. Let's leave him alone. He'll manage to get into her room tonight, and tomorrow he won't give her another thought.

C

COUNTESS (*moving to* L *of Hortensia*) Hortensia, you're blind. Tiger isn't the same any more. Something has been touched in him that nothing has been able to reach before. (*She moves down* C *and faces front*) I was watching him yesterday during dinner; he looked like a snapshot of himself one of his comrades took during the war, the morning of the German offensive; a little boy, standing perfectly happily beside his cannon. I didn't think anything but death could bring back that look to his face. Hortensia, I tell you he's in love with that girl.

HORTENSIA. Tiger is incapable of love.

COUNTESS (*moving up* LC) I tell you, he's in the process of learning. You may do as you please: I shall never put up with it. (*She turns to Hortensia*) Were things successful with you physically?

HORTENSIA. You embarrass me, Eliane.

COUNTESS. My dear Hortensia, this isn't the time to be prudish. We have to protect ourselves. Was he always very amorous?

HORTENSIA. Tiger is a wonderful lover.

COUNTESS. That's what they all tell me. But after all, there are degrees of success. (*She crosses above Hortensia and stands down* R) Tiger catches fire, in an instant, at sight of a supple figure. The only secret of beauty, he insists, is the way a fine bust is borne above a slender waist, with real hips below. I've known him follow gipsies for hours in the street—(*she crosses to the settee*) women reeking of goats and stale tobacco. He swore they were princesses, the only women who knew how to walk. I don't know what miracle kept him from having his throat cut by their pimps ten times over. (*She sits on the settee*) I tell you all this simply to show you how strong his desires are. But I know him. He's not the man to live on aesthetic considerations. Hortensia, let us put our cards on the table. Was it successful between the two of you, on that level?

HORTENSIA. Dear Eliane, would you like details?

COUNTESS. No, thank you. That particular activity of Tiger's interests me as much as his passion for polo. But when he comes home from a match, I can ask him quite frankly if his horse disappointed him—in his love affairs, I have always stopped at speculation. This time I need to know.

HORTENSIA. I don't think his horse disappoints him.

COUNTESS. Good. That's important. He hasn't touched that child yet. She's a virgin, that sticks out a mile, probably clumsy and without flair. If he does make an incursion into the west wing, he may come straight back to us, utterly deflated. He has a morbid horror of failure.

HORTENSIA. Eliane, it's my turn to find your feelings limited. Love, even restricted to that, is an infinitely more subtle game than polo. The heart may very well mingle itself with the pleasures of the flesh in an unexpected fashion. I can only speak by hearsay; but I imagine that a tender feeling for a new little person who gives herself clumsily, might teach Tiger a host of new joys—even beyond desire, or perhaps subtly fused with desire.

COUNTESS. I don't like a woman to know too well what her lover may feel with another. On my own level, where I know I have remained Tiger's wife, on the level of intelligence and our mutual tastes in life, I feel instinctively there's a chance he may escape me. That's quite enough. I must act. With or without you.

HORTENSIA. With me, of course. What do you take me for? I'm interested in nothing at the moment but getting Tiger back, even if I leave him next morning.

COUNTESS. Do both, my dear, and I'll be much obliged. In the intervals between two mistresses, Tiger is an entrancing husband. He usually feels the need to take me travelling and pay discreet court to me—all very platonic, naturally—but I have never been wildly sensual. (*She rises and moves up* R) I shall profit by the occasion to leave Villebosse, who is beginning to bore me. It will be divine.

HORTENSIA. Eliane, I'm delighted to assist your honeymoon with all the modest means at my disposal. Where will you go—Italy?

COUNTESS. That's very overdone. That's where Tiger took me the first time, when I still believed in the moon. It might remind me of my disappointments. Tiger is dying to go to Japan. He who yawns his way round the world, tells me it's the only country for which he feels the least interest.

HORTENSIA. Japan is a charming idea. Let's set to work on your trip to Japan. How shall we go about it?

COUNTESS (*moving to* L *of Hortensia*) Dear little Hortensia. (*She takes Hortensia's hand and raises her from the chair*) Let me kiss you. (*She kisses her*) Tell me whether, in your heart of hearts, you really care for him so little? You aren't going to play me the dirty trick of leaving him stuck with that child? I have the impression I dropped my guard a little while I was talking to you just now.

HORTENSIA (*embracing her*) Dear Eliane! I should be delighted to play you some little mischief of that sort. I shall never forgive you for staying friends with Tiger all the time he has been my lover. But don't worry; my pride is stronger than my feelings. I can't allow him to leave me for that little trollop. I propose to do the leaving myself. I shall reserve my revenge on you for some other time.

(*They mutually embrace*)

COUNTESS. What a dear it is. (*She crosses to* LC) Now listen. I have a very simple plan I want to tell you about. (*She turns to Hortensia*) That little ninny is bound to be full of prejudice and wounded pride. I shall say I've been robbed of a jewel—I shall have all the servants' rooms searched—her own included. Afterwards, it can be found— on one of the garden paths, or under a sofa cushion—that's a mere detail. (*She crosses to the door down* R, *opens it and stands aside*) But it might be enough to drive her away.

(HORTENSIA *crosses to the door down* R)

It's quite extraordinary, my dear, how sensitive the poor can be.

(HORTENSIA *exits down* R.

The COUNTESS *follows her off. There is a brief pause.*

The COUNT *and* HERO *enter down* L. *The* COUNT *stands up* LC)

HERO (*crossing to* R) Do we rehearse or do we not, as Villebosse says? I can just about bear my waistcoat for three acts, not more. Thank God the French classics are short. If you'd insisted on giving one of Victor Hugo's dramas, I should have exploded long before the end, scattering my liver like a shower of poisoned flowers over the guests. What a splendid exit for a drunk.

COUNT. Hero, I'm not enjoying it any more.

HERO. You're tired of Marivaux? Thank God for that. All the same, you're not asking us to change the play? I was so pleased with my part. A lord! "What are you playing, my dear Hero?" "A lord." It sounded discreet and mysterious, and there weren't too many lines to remember.

COUNT. It doesn't amuse me any more to amuse myself.

HERO. You've taken long enough to find that out. I discovered the remedy twenty years ago. (*He moves to the table up* C) Have a drink. (*He pours a drink for himself*)

COUNT. It wouldn't amuse me to get drunk. (*He moves above the settee*)

HERO. Do you suppose one gets drunk to amuse oneself? If you knew the care and perseverance it takes. Always emptying glasses and filling them up again. People take you for a rich idler, when all you are is a bottle-washer. I've got an idea. Work.

COUNT. It's a bad habit which must be learnt very young. Besides, I don't believe it would amuse me.

HERO (*crossing to the armchair, glass in hand, and sitting*) Do as I do, make love. Change your women. It's not so hilarious as it sounds, but at least it helps to keep hope alive.

COUNT. I have tried it—not as much as you, but I've tried. Let me tell you, taking it all in all, I don't believe it's an occupation for a man.

HERO. You're depressing me. How old are you?

COUNT (*moving behind the settee*) A year older than you. You've known that ever since I joined you at school a year late. We owe our friendship to my scarlet fever.

HERO. You're not suppressing a desire to dedicate your life to some useful purpose?

COUNT. Certainly not. I know what that means, too.

HERO. Nor a sudden passion for making money? With Eliane's fortune it would be quite immoral and in very bad taste.

COUNT. I hate money.

HERO. No big words. Despise it, that's enough.

COUNT (*crossing above the settee to* C) Imagine, Hero, that one day everything suddenly fell into place and became simple and peaceful —but at the same time, inaccessible.

HERO. I haven't much imagination. Wait while I transpose.

Alcohol is suddenly prescribed by my doctors as the elixir of life, but at that precise moment, all the bars I know are closed.

Count. That's right. (*He moves to* R *of the settee*) Except that there is one bar open, just one. A poor little provincial café where you'd never dream of going.

Hero. There's no such thing as a poor little provincial café where I'd never dream of going.

Count. All the same, you go in by accident, or design, and once over the threshold, you discover that life is vastly more simple, very much more serious—and very much better than you ever thought it could be.

Hero. These analogies dredged up from the drink-trade are sometimes obscure and in very doubtful taste. Besides, they're making me thirsty. (*He rises, moves to the table up* C *and refills his glass*) Enough of parables. You're in love.

Count. Yes.

Hero (*moving to* R *of the Count*) Good. It can't be serious. You've told me that at least ten times before.

Count. So I have. Very well, I am not in love.

Hero. Then it's real? You've told me that at least three times before—on two occasions with tears. (*He moves to* R *of the table up* C)

Count. All right, have it your own way—this time it isn't real. Because it's like nothing I have ever known before. (*He sits on the settee*)

(Hero *looks at the Count while he picks up the decanter*)

Hero (*suddenly; in another voice*) You disgust me.

Count. Why?

Hero (*gently*) I don't like the way you look. (*He refills his glass*)

Count. Am I ugly?

Hero (*crossing down* R) You're beautiful. You look as you did at Sainte-Barbe when we were fifteen—(*he crosses to* L) in the days before we climbed the wall together to visit a brothel.

(*The* Count *rises and crosses above the armchair to* R *of it*)

As you did when we came back from football in winter, hot, flushed, sweating, muddy and whistling after the girls. (*He moves above the settee*) As you did that night in the dormitory when we swore eternal friendship, and hacked away at our arms with a little rusty penknife to mingle our blood. (*In a low voice*) Don't play me that trick, Tiger, I should never fogive you.

Count. It took us an hour to carve ourselves up. What cowards we were. Do you remember the vow?

Hero (*harshly*) No.

Count (*moving to Hero*) I could say it for you. I came across it last night, quite by chance.

Hero (*sitting on the settee at the upstage end*) No. I don't want to remember. Don't do this to me, Tiger. Look, my hands are shaking, I'm a miserable wreck, in a year or two at most they'll either trundle me away in a bathchair, or I'll be dead. I couldn't bear for you to become him again now.

COUNT. Become whom?

HERO (*brutally*) You know. (*He grips the glass in his hand so tightly, it breaks*)

(*They both look at the glass*)

(*Gently*) I'm sorry, dear boy. I like to break things.

COUNT (*looking at Hero's hand*) You're mad! You're bleeding. (*He hands his handkerchief to Hero*) You've been looking on the wine when it's red.

HERO. Wine is always red, let me tell you. You should learn that. (*He holds out a piece of glass*)

(*The* COUNT *takes the pieces of glass and moves* C)

Cut yourself, Tiger, and let us swear an oath.

COUNT. What oath?

HERO. That we're both content with each other as we are, and we'll go on bravely amusing ourselves to the end. (*He rises and moves down* L, *wiping his hand*) If you're tired of Hortensia, take another mistress. If you're short of money, I'll keep you supplied. If you want to forget, I'll teach you to drink. But enjoy yourself as I do, Tiger, please. And don't look like that any more.

COUNT (*moving down* R) I can't help it. What can I do?

HERO (*crossing to the Count*) We all have to choose, Tiger. And we have chosen. It's too late. (*He moves to the table up* C *and pours a fresh drink. With a change of tone*) Besides, it would grieve me, dear fellow, to see you make an ass of yourself.

COUNT (*moving up* R; *after a pause*) You've never forgiven me for Evangeline, have you?

HERO (*moving to* R *of the settee*) No.

COUNT (*moving down* RC) But, my dear boy, it was no sort of marriage for you. You were nineteen. You would have buried yourself, you . . . (*He breaks off*) Forgive me. Today, for the first time, I see I might have been wrong when I stopped you marrying that girl.

HERO. What's done is done. You weren't wrong. We've had plenty of fun together, since then. No regrets. Between my six children, my wife and my gun dogs, in some little provincial château, I should most certainly have come to the same end, somewhat less brilliantly, that's all. No, no, no, my dear fellow. In our family, we are drunkards from father to son, just as in other families they're all upholsterers. But one good piece of advice deserves another—leave what they call love alone. It's not for us.

COUNT. If you love me, you should want me to be happy.

HERO. Not any more. Not in that way. Besides, we shouldn't cling to our illusions, either of us. We haven't loved each other for twenty years—not since we went into long trousers. That doesn't prevent us being good friends. (*He moves up* c) Let's drink together, Tiger. Amuse yourself how you like.

(*The* Count *crosses and stands above the settee*)

After all, you are free. But no more confidences. Besides, one mustn't hope too much, not any more. (*He moves down* R) Life takes pains to put things in order and keep them that way. Life's an orderly business.

Count (*moving down* c) We shall see.

Hero (*moving up* c) We shall see. One always sees. That's what's so marvellous in the human condition.

(*The* Countess *and* Hortensia *enter down* R. *The* Count *crosses to* L)

We cry "Eureka" five minutes before we die, and the curtain falls on that consoling word. (*He refills his glass and stands up* R) Good afternoon, Eliane.

Countess (*crossing to the Count*) Tiger, I'm very upset. I must speak to you. My emerald ring has disappeared.

(Hortensia *crosses above the armchair to* L *of the table up* c)

Count. Ask your maid to look for it, my dear. Not me—I have a horror of such exercises. You prick your fingers on the sofa cushions fill your nails with dirt, and disinter an ancient letter, which always makes unpleasant reading—when it isn't a bill. (*He turns and puts the pieces of glass on the table* L)

Countess. We've been searching all the morning. I had it yesterday. In this room. I left it in the cloakroom, where we keep our costumes, because I thought the green didn't go with my dress. I'm very upset. I'm afraid someone may have behaved badly.

Count. Now, no nonsense. Look in the cloakroom again.

Countess. Of course. But if I don't find it, I ought to tell the insurance people. They'll come down to make enquiries. It will be odious.

Count. After the ball, my dear, after the ball. You don't expect me to clap your minions of the law into Louis Quinze costumes, hoping nobody will notice them? After the ball, please.

Countess. I'm sorry, Tiger, but the insurance people must be notified within twenty-four hours. I shall go and search again. (*She turns and moves up* c) Hero, will you help me?

Hero (*moving to the door down* R) Delighted to be of use. It must be my first chance in thirty-seven years.

(Hero *exits down* R.
    The Countess *follows him off*)

Count (*calling after the Countess*) But no fuss, I implore you. (*To* Hortensia) My dear, one's whole life is poisoned by fear of burglars and shipwrecks and, if, in fact, you question your friends, no-one has ever been robbed and the ship has never gone down. (*He crosses to the armchair and sits*)

HORTENSIA (*moving to the Count*) This ring business is most annoying.

COUNT. Of course it's annoying. (*He takes Hortensia's hand and holds it against his face*) But really, Eliane has so many jewels, she can afford to lose one now and again. Besides, it would be immoral if it was always the same woman who wore them.

HORTENSIA. I'm sure Eliane is taking it less cheerfully. It was an admirable stone. She means to search all the servants' rooms.

COUNT. Now, all the servants have been with the family for twenty years. Surely if they were going to steal from her they'd have done it already. Her own maid's younger, of course, but then she's her goddaughter: she was littered like the kittens in the kitchen. Besides, she spends her entire time going to mass. Unless she wanted to buy candles, I really don't see why the trinket should interest her. (*He releases her hand*)

HORTENSIA. Well, Eliane has decided to search the whole house. It seems the most elementary precaution. (*She moves to the settee*) Now, who else is here, besides the servants? Villebosse, Hero—(*she sits on the settee at the upstage end*) Monsieur Damiens, me . . .

COUNT (*interrupting*) My dear, I abominate detective stories. I think they're the most futile things in the world. (*He rises and moves to her*) If I ever happen to open one in bed, after a disappointing evening, I always drop off to sleep before the villain is unmasked. And I'm never interested enough to open the book again next morning. I don't believe one should look for criminals in life, either. (*He crosses down* R) Either everyone's guilty, or nobody is.

HORTENSIA. Your taste for paradox threatens to lead you astray, Tiger. I don't think Eliane's is as developed as yours. If I know anything about her, she'll have all the rooms in the west wing searched, as she said she would.

COUNT (*a little sharply*) If Eliane has the west wing searched, I shall insist on the east wing being searched as well. I shall lose my watch, my dear—(*he crosses to her*) and hide it in your bedroom. (*He looks at her, hard*) Did you think up this little story together? I congratulate you.

HORTENSIA (*suddenly very innocent*) What story, Tiger?

COUNT (*drawing Hortensia to her feet; squarely*) Hortensia, I loved you once. It's too grand a word, of course, but we have so few that we must group a good many sentiments under the same heading. My hands, in any case, have loved you. Every time we met, I knew a sort of joy, very pure—yes, it's strange, very pure—and very close to happiness—in touching you.

HORTENSIA. Thank you, Tiger.

COUNT. Don't thank me. It has nothing to do with you, no doubt. I'm going to pay you a compliment, Hortensia, the first and probably the last—(*he kisses her hand*) you're very beautiful. I don't mean your face; that's charming, of course, but I don't much believe in faces. Besides, with the universal fashion for cosmetics, all women who aren't positively ugly, look alike. But your body is very beautiful noble and beautiful, like an animal's. And in all true beauty there is something solemn. If God exists, such beauty must reflect something of Himself.

HORTENSIA. Good God!

COUNT. Yes. An odd word in my mouth. Believe me, I'm quite conscious of sounding absurd when I say it. But the memory of the day I held you in my arms for the first time is as clear and dazzling as a memory of my childhood: the first palace my father showed me in Italy. The same stab of pain and the same joy. (*He crosses down* R) Eliane's a woman of intellect, but I rate that low; it's the weapon of the poor. Leave intellect to play her ugly little game alone—as for you, stay out of it. Be worthy of your beauty. Beauty's a great lady.

HORTENSIA. This must be a new game, Tiger, you don't usually talk so gravely. You're scaring me.

COUNT. I'm scaring myself a little. Do you think it amuses me to be so far out of my depth? (*He crosses to the table up* C, *takes a cigar from a box, and lights it*) I'm not used to it: any minute now, I expect to start gasping for air.

HORTENSIA (*sitting on the settee*) Tiger, that child isn't even pretty. She's shrewd and docile, but she doesn't even know how to behave. She will shame you by her little nursemaid's frock, the first time you take her out, and if you try to dress her up, she'll shame you even more; I know you.

COUNT (*moving down* C) I'm foolish enough to feel ashamed, it's true. But that has nothing to do with it.

HORTENSIA. You belong to a different world, Tiger. The head and the heart commit a thousand follies; the hands are rarely mistaken. I'm sure you still want me.

COUNT (*smiling at her; gently*) Of course I do. I'm capable of anything. Only, you see, I love her.

HORTENSIA. Really, Tiger, it's absurd. She's the opposite of everything you could love.

COUNT. The opposite. Exactly. And I love her. It's comic, don't you think?

HORTENSIA (*bursting out laughing*) Oh, it's too stupid. It's really too stupid. Forgive me, but I assure you, it's too stupid.

COUNT. Yes, it is stupid. This adventure is making me wholly stupid. (*He moves to her*) But I couldn't bear never to have felt like this.

(DAMIENS *enters down* R)

DAMIENS (*moving to* R *of the armchair*) Monsieur le Comte, Madame la Comtesse has just discovered the loss of an emerald ring. She has ordered her butler and steward to search the bedrooms in the west wing. You gave me assurance of the respect you intended to have shown to my goddaughter in this house. Will you allow her room to be searched?

COUNT. Certainly not, Monsieur Damiens. (*He crosses to the door down* R) Come with me. We'll put an end to this charade.

> (*The* COUNT *exits down* R.
> DAMIENS *follows him off*.
> VILLEBOSSE *enters up* R)

VILLEBOSSE (*moving above the armchair*) Once and for all, do we rehearse or do we not? We've been dressed for the last two hours.

HORTENSIA. But we're all acting, Villebosse. We're in the thick of a comedy. (*She crosses to the door down* R) Haven't you noticed yet?

> (HORTENSIA *sweeps out down* R.
> HERO *enters down* L, *leaving the door open*)

VILLEBOSSE. I swear they're all laughing at me. (*To Hero*) Sir!

HERO. Sir?

VILLEBOSSE. Everyone in this house is laughing at me.

HERO (*moving to the table up* C) That's quite possible, sir. (*He pours a drink for himself*)

VILLEBOSSE (*moving to* R *of the table up* C) Sir, I have the impression that you're at the bottom of this distasteful behaviour.

HERO (*picking up his glass and crossing towards the door down* L) That's equally possible, sir.

VILLEBOSSE (*following Hero*) What would you say, sir, if I insisted on reparation?

HERO. Sir, I love to break, but I never repair.

> (HERO *exits down* L)

VILLEBOSSE (*shouting after Hero*) Sir, you have refused my challenge. I shall publish it everywhere. I'll cover you with shame.

> (*The* COUNTESS, *beside herself, enters down* R *and crosses to* C)

COUNTESS. Villebosse!

VILLEBOSSE (*crossing to* L *of the Countess*) Eliane, my love . . .

COUNTESS. Tiger has just insulted me unbearably. One of my jewels has been stolen. When I told the servants to search the rooms in the west wing, he forbade them to enter the room of that little brat he's forced on us all for the last week. He's sworn that if they search her room, they must search mine first. He claims that I have not lost the ring, but hidden it. (*She moves up* C) It's insulting. His behaviour's been utterly caddish.

VILLEBOSSE (*crossing to the door down* R *and turning*) I won't tolerate it, Eliane. Allow me to challenge him.

COUNTESS (*moving down* RC) Will you never understand anything? There's no question of challenging Tiger because he's failed in respect for me. It's his right: after all, I am his wife. It's a question of impressing on him that he's making a fool of me by flaunting himself with that little nobody of a nursemaid. If he takes her back to Paris, Villebosse, I shan't dare to show my face the entire winter.

VILLEBOSSE. It's intolerable. I shall settle everything. Count on me.

(VILLEBOSSE *exits down* R.
LUCILE *enters down* L. *She carries a door key*)

LUCILE (*crossing to the Countess and holding out the key*) I have brought you the key of my room, madame. I want it to be searched with all the others. Besides, they may well find the ring there, and then everyone will feel much better.

COUNTESS (*sitting in the armchair*) My dear child, I don't know what you're talking about. My maid is still searching my own room and my husband is helping her. It is, of course, quite possible that I have put the ring away somewhere and forgotten about it.

LUCILE. That would be good news.

COUNTESS. Yes. Suspicions are always horrid for everyone. I'm so sorry if I've hurt your feelings. It was merely a general measure that concerned the whole staff.

(LUCILE *moves to* L *of the Countess and again offers the key*)

I expect you've come to tell me you want to give up your part in the play. Perhaps you don't even want to go on looking after the children? The poor little souls had grown so fond of you already, everyone tells me. Do think it over. I'm sure it will break their hearts. But if your decision is unshakeable, I think the best thing would be to act as quickly and as brutally as possible. There's a train in about an hour. The car can take you to the station as soon as your bag is packed.

(LUCILE *moves below the settee*)

I know the decision is yours. I shall pay you six months' wages. I know how awkwardly you're placed.

(*The* COUNT *enters down* R *and crosses to* R *of the Countess*)

(*She turns to the Count, very much at ease*) Tiger, mademoiselle tells me she's leaving us. I'm terribly sorry about your play, but in three days we can easily replace her. I told her that so far as the children were concerned, it would be much better to go away at once. They're immensely attached to her already, as we all are, but we mustn't risk having them make an even worse fuss later on.

COUNT (*handing a ring to the Countess*) Eliane, here is your emerald. (*He crosses above the armchair to* L *of the Countess*)

COUNTESS (*putting the ring on her finger*) Oh, how splendid. Where was it?

COUNT. In your own room. Under one of the candlesticks.

COUNTESS. Heavens! Why on earth did I put it there?

COUNT (*moving up* LC) Now I must ask you to apologize to mademoiselle.

COUNTESS. Apologize? What for? Yes, of course. I am distressed at my stupidity, mademoiselle. I hope you'll forgive me and not carry away too unhappy a memory of this house. I am sure you will agree, Tiger, that we should give the child six months' wages.

COUNT (*moving down* c) My dear Eliane, you know I never allow any inconvenience to interfere with an entertainment, once I've decided to give it. We can neither cancel the performance nor recast the part in three days. Please be good enough to see that mademoiselle retracts her decision.

COUNTESS. Indeed, I've said all I could, Tiger. Her feelings are hurt. She insists on going. And I must admit I understand how she feels.

COUNT (*crossing below the Countess to* R *of her*) I'm sure there's still something you can say. I count on this small diplomatic success on your part, Eliane, or you'll disappoint me exceedingly. (*He looks directly at Lucile*) I'll leave you together. (*He looks directly at the Countess*) In half an hour's time, we rehearse.

(*The* COUNT *exits down* R. LUCILE *still says nothing*)

COUNTESS. There now! It seems I must induce you to stay, under pain of quarrelling with Tiger to the death. You're very young, mademoiselle. When the time comes to choose, never fall in love with a frivolous man.

LUCILE (*gently*) Are you in love with him?

COUNTESS. What a question, mademoiselle. He's my husband.

LUCILE. Do you think he can be happy amusing himself all the time?

COUNTESS. My dear child, don't expect me to allow our interview —since apparently we must have one—to take on that tone. I have a horror of familiarities. Tiger has begged me to ask you to stay. I am asking you. If he has to cancel this performance, he will make himself ill. Besides, why should you go? As soon as the entertainment is over, we shall return to Paris, for the season. So everything will slip back into place, isn't that so? (*She rises and moves* c) Come, mademoiselle, forgive me for this little incident. Tiger would be capable of sulking with me for a whole week if he felt you were still vexed with me. (*She moves* RC) You and I know very little of each other; but you must appreciate the respect I have for your godfather, Monsieur Damiens. Now there's a man who's extremely fond of you.

LUCILE (*facing front*) Yes. So he tells me.

COUNTESS. He has suffered a great deal, too, I believe. He's been separated from his wife for years, hasn't he? And even during their life together, she doesn't seem to have brought him the comfort he might have expected. He quite astonishes one by the sensibility hidden under that rather stern exterior. (*She sits in the armchair*) He talked to me about you at great length.

LUCILE. Really?

COUNTESS. Yes. You know, I like you. You're really so young, so defenceless with your little air of knowing everything. I'm sure that under all that high-mindedness, you're more than willing to burn your wings like a delicate insect at the first candle that comes your way. You say to yourself—(*she rises and stands above the armchair*) "Won't it be beautiful. At last it will be the life I've always dreamed of." For a week you live in that dream, and afterwards, you're left with only your eyes to weep with. Damiens told me you were proud and poor. That's a great virtue, with a very great defect. (*She moves* c) When a girl's fastidious, pretty, clever and penniless, she's always a little *déclassée*. Think it over. Damiens is a man of honour, and still very good-looking. I can speak to you as a woman who knows what life is, who is very much older than you are, and who would be miserable—really miserable—to see you throwing away your beautiful youth for some folly with no future in it. When a girl is alone in the world, her first thought must be for the future. (*She moves* R) Heavens! I know it can't be much fun—at twenty, one has all sorts of other dreams—but that's the way the world goes, my dear. We can do nothing about it. (*She pauses and looks at Lucile. Suddenly*) Damiens, who is my friend, has served us long and faithfully. May I say, that in my eyes, it would be as if you had become his wife. (*She crosses to Lucile*) In fact, this very emerald would be my wedding present. (*She removes the ring and holds it out to Lucile*)

(LUCILE *takes the ring, looks at it for an instant then returns it to the Countess*)

LUCILE. It's too beautiful a present for that kind of ceremony. No, thank you, madame.

COUNTESS. You're making a mistake. It was sincerely meant.

LUCILE. Besides, whether in that way or the other, I shall never marry. I have sworn it.

COUNTESS (*turning away* R) How can you possibly tell, at your age? When did you make this bold decision?

LUCILE (*gently*) Last night.

COUNTESS. Very well. When you see Tiger again, I shall be obliged if you'll tell him that I did all I could.

LUCILE. I'll tell him, madame.

(LUCILE *turns and exits down* L, *leaving the door open. The* COUNTESS *moves up* C, *thinking, then crosses to the window up* L, *looks out and calls to Hero*)

COUNTESS. Hero! Hero! No, not you, Villebosse. Hero. Come up here at once. I want to talk to you.

(HERO *enters up* L, *glass in hand*)

(*She moves to the armchair*) Hero. We must stop Tiger making a fool of himself.

(HERO *crosses to the Countess*)

He's in love with that child. She's been his mistress since last night and she's told him she loves him. It's ludicrous and it's mad. I don't know if you've noticed him this last week?

HERO (*impassively*) Oh, yes, I've noticed.

COUNTESS. It's revolting.

HERO (*moving below the settee*) It is revolting. So I told him.

COUNTESS. Are you on my side, Hero?

(HERO *glances at her then raises his glass*)

Then do something. Only you can do something, I'm sure of that.

HERO. Do something with him? But Tiger is impenetrably kind . . .

COUNTESS. With her, perhaps.

HERO (*declaiming*)

"And what commandment do you lay upon me?
To please that woman and become her lover?"

COUNTESS. Well, you could, Hero, if you put your mind to it. The child's a crazy romantic, no better than a shopgirl, probably worse. Everyone knows you're irresistible. (*She moves to him*) Seduce her.

HERO. There's only one difficulty. This girl isn't everyone. She doesn't know I'm irresistible. (*He crosses to* R) That cuts out half my chances.

COUNTESS. Nonsense! She'll burst with satisfaction, like any other girl, when the two most brilliant men of the party pay attention to no-one but her. In two days' time, you and Tiger will become confused in her mind. I know these little Puritans. I was like that myself before Tiger married me.

(HERO *gives her a look*)

Women are women, my dear, always even when they give themselves the airs of angels. Hero, I don't have to tell you what to do. (*She crosses to him*) Give her a few drinks one evening, swear you love her. Add a little moonlight and music, and the little ninny will believe you. At least, she'll believe you enough to surrender herself for one night. (*She crosses below the settee to* L) Afterwards, Tiger will throw her over, or if he agrees to share her, the real danger will be over.

HERO. You're doing me a great honour, Eliane, in being so certain no-one can resist me. I'd say yes, for any grown woman, even if she didn't know what everyone knows. After all, I'm a professional—but an innocent young girl—oh, no. (*He moves to the table up* C) They're very strange creatures, and I haven't had much to do with them.

COUNTESS. I tell you she's no longer innocent. She's his mistress.

HERO (*picking up the decanter*) Since last night. She'll keep her state of grace a little longer. (*He refills his glass*)

COUNTESS (*moving to* L *of the table up* C) Then you'll allow Tiger to make a complete fool of himself? Swamp himself in ridicule? He loves her, Hero, he loves her, I'm sure of it. Don't you care whether he's in love, just like an adolescent boy?

HERO (*suddenly very hard*) You're wrong. I do care. (*He moves down R, glass in hand*)

COUNTESS. Are you afraid of hurting him? Of breaking both their hearts?

HERO. It's not that, either. I told you: I like to break things.

COUNTESS (*moving C*) She sleeps alone, at the end of the west wing. It isn't certain you could seduce her, assuming she really loves him. And if he loves her, too. Tiger might intervene, carry her away. But we all know you're a brute. You're mad for the child. (*She crosses to him*) As usual, you've been drinking, You force her door. I'll see that the lock's out of order. (*She puts her hand on his shoulder and strokes his hair, etc.*) Of course she'll cry for help, but she's miles out of earshot there, and besides, what can a young girl do with her nails, her feeble fists, her tears, against the desires of a grown man? (*She crosses down L*) If she loves him she'll run away next morning, out of pure shame.

(*There is a silence*)

HERO (*softly*) Evangeline!

COUNTESS (*turning to him*) What was that?

HERO. The name of a young girl. You must have met her. She married a banker—Blumenstein. She was very beautiful. Her marriage was unhappy and she died.

COUNTESS. A slim young thing, fair, with wonderful great eyes? Like a sacrificial faun? She was presented to me at the Rothschilds. But where's the connection?

HERO. Very slight and very far away. I'm glad you remember her. Come, Eliane, they'll be here in a moment to rehearse. This play has got to be well acted, no matter what happens. Like all trifles, it's immensely important.

(*The* COUNTESS *moves to the table up C and pauses, thinking*)

Her husband was a swine.

(*The* COUNTESS *picks up a fan from the table*)

It was even said that he beat her.

COUNTESS (*moving down LC and turning*) I've had an idea.

(HERO *moves to the table up C and puts down his glass*)

I shall arrange for a telegram to be sent to Tiger, calling him away tonight.

They smile at each other. HERO *crosses below the Countess and exits down* L.

The COUNTESS *follows him off, fanning herself as—*

the CURTAIN *falls*

ACT III

SCENE 1

SCENE—*Lucile's small attic bedroom. The same night.*
    The door is L. *A small bed stands with its head against the wall* R.
*Below the bed there is a small table with an oil lamp on it and below the
table, down* R, *there is an old trunk on its side, with a dress flung over it.
There is a washstand up* LC *with jug, basin, etc., and another oil lamp.
A wooden chair stands down* L, *below the door. Lucile's dress and coat
hang on the back of the door.*

When the CURTAIN *rises,* LUCILE, *in her dressing-gown, is lying on the bed,
reading. The door opens softly.* LUCILE *looks up, surprised.* HERO *enters.
He is still in his costume, his jabot slightly awry. He carries two glasses
and a decanter half-filled with brandy.* LUCILE *sits up.*

HERO (*smiling*) Don't be afraid. Tiger's just telephoned to say he
won't be back till late tonight. He asked me to give you the message
and keep you company for a while. (*He comes further into the room,
leaving the door ajar*)

    (LUCILE *rises and stands below the bed*)

May I sit down?
    LUCILE (*pointing to the chair down* L) Yes.
    HERO (*looking at the chair*) How very odd, when there are so many
comfortable chairs in this château. I suppose they didn't cater for
visitors in the west wing. You take the bed, my angel, you'll be more
comfortable. Have a little drink?
    LUCILE. No.
    HERO. Your mistake. (*He fills one glass, then puts both glasses and
the decanter on the washstand*) You don't mind if I help myself? In my
present state, it would be unwise of me to stop. I should be drunk in
a flash and behave very badly. If I drink a little more, I postpone
the hour of reckoning. You won't be bored if I chat with you for
a little? (*He picks up the empty glass and the decanter and moves* LC, *filling
the glass*) When the others sleep, I begin my long solitary struggle till
dawn, when at last I can shut an eye. Damn that eye! There it is,
open wide again, taking in everything. Everything bores it stiff, too,
but it goes on staring, stubborn little devil. Even if I'm dying for
sleep, even if I've been wide awake for twenty-four hours. (*He puts
the decanter on the floor in front of the chair, picks up a book from the chair,
then sits on the chair, his glass in one hand, the book in the other*) In the
daytime, I can manage all right. I drink a little, I talk a little—never
mind what I talk about. The sound of my own voice keeps me from
thinking. But when the rest of you are all safely in bed, then I start

to think, and that's horrible. Would you be good enough to stop me thinking a little?

(LUCILE *slips her feet into her slippers*)

Besides, it's Tiger's express orders. He told me, "Go up and tell her I shan't be coming home and keep her company for a bit."

(*There is a silence*)

(*He smiles*) He must have hoped you'd speak to me from time to time.

LUCILE (*sitting on the end of the bed*) What would you like me to say?

HERO. I don't know. Something pleasant. That you're mistaken: that it isn't Tiger you're in love with, but me.

(LUCILE *smiles, but does not reply*)

Then tell me you love Tiger—it won't be such pleasant hearing, of course, but better than nothing.

LUCILE. I can't believe he wanted us to talk of that. I can't believe he has discussed me with you.

HERO. Ah, my child! You don't know men. Inveterate gossips: we tell each other everything.

LUCILE. Are you very fond of him?

HERO. We were throwing stink bombs at girls before you dreamed of entering the world, dear baby. We even mingled our blood one night in the dormitory. For life and for death. The occasion of dying for each other didn't present itself immediately, that's all. And since then, we've had to live. Yes, we're very fond of each other and none of the women in our lives has managed to come between us.

LUCILE (*asking like a child*) Has he had lots of women?

HERO (*smiling*) Dear baby! He adores you, of course, but you must admit it would have been a,most unwise gamble on his part to have waited for you. Does it hurt you very much, to think he's had other women?

LUCILE. That's my secret.

HERO. You keep it, my precious, with your little handkerchief tucked in on top. (*He puts the book on the floor below his chair*) Personally, I'm not much interested in confidences. They're always more or less the same, and only comfort the one who does the confessing. You are young, you're on your voyage to Cythera; you must feel like an explorer, a discoverer of new continents. It's very charming. You'll soon realize that the play has only two or three characters, two or three situations eternally repeated—and that what springs from the heart in the greatest moments of ecstasy is never more than a stale platitude. There's nothing new to invent. And that includes our vices which are revoltingly banal and commonplace. A whole catalogue, with the market-price in the right-hand column. For everything has to be paid for, of course. Alcoholism—gout and cirrhosis of the liver. Drug-taking—police courts and a high tax on

D

one's pleasure. Passion—fatigue. True love—a dear little broken heart. And no discount for cash. (*He refills his glass*)

LUCILE (*looking squarely at him; gently*) I've loved Tiger since yesterday, and I'm twenty. So your little lecture is a waste of time.

HERO (*rising and bowing; the decanter in one hand, the glass in the other*) Touché! Congratulations. (*He moves to her*) There was only one answer you could give to my drunkard's disenchantment, and you found it at once. What a lucky fellow Tiger is. He's brought this off, too. He succeeds in everything, whether it's horse-racing or love.

LUCILE. What's he succeeded in?

HERO. In finding you. I must confess that when I came into this room just now, like everyone else in this house, I still took you for one of those little shopgirls in the agony columns who's had a tiff with her sweetheart. You snubbed me. Splendid! (*He puts the decanter on the left end of the washstand*) That'll teach me to look at girls a little more closely in future. (*He moves the chair, and puts it in front of the washstand, facing* L) Now we can meet——

(LUCILE *rises and moves* R, *below the bed*)

—on equal terms and gossip away like old friends. You know, it was a stroke of genius to make everyone take you for an insignificant little mouse.

LUCILE. I am insignificant and I can't string three words together. I don't know how he managed to make me talk at all.

HERO. Tiger is good at everything. I'll bet you were a virgin before.

(LUCILE *does not reply. She sits on the downstage side of the bed*)

(*He sits on the chair with his back to Lucile*) Here we go! I've hurt her feelings. Are we friends or are we not? Do have just one glass with me. If I'm the only one drinking, we'll never get down to conversation.

LUCILE. No, thank you, sir.

HERO (*laughingly repeating*) "No, thank you, sir!" Polite, too. Neat as a new pin. A fine little pebble all bright and shiny, that monsieur found on the beach without even looking for it, strolling with his hands in his pockets and his nose in the air, as always. I tell you, he has too much luck, it's maddening.

(HERO's *tone surprises* LUCILE *a little*)

(*He corrects himself*) It really is, you know; or anyway, it would madden me if I didn't happen to be so fond of him. But he'll find out that I do love him—not, of course, in the same way as you do— but very much, all the same, and that I can forgive him anything. Let's talk about him, shall we? It will be pleasant and perhaps I shall go to sleep later on. (*He rises*) Sure you won't have a drop?

LUCILE. No.

HERO. No? (*He turns to face her and sits astride the chair*) Well, never mind. What made you give yourself to him, all at once like that, for the very first time? After all, you didn't even know him yesterday.

(LUCILE *does not reply*)

I don't pry into secrets. All the same, it must have been so delightful
—all of a sudden. It's something so far outside my own experience,
it might even convert me. No? You don't want to tell me about it?
I'll never know then, even by hearsay, how love is set in motion?

LUCILE (*after a pause; softly, as if to herself*) I could never bear
anyone to touch me. And yet, when he took me in his arms, I felt
I had come to the end of a journey. (*She leans a little towards Hero*)
That's all. I wasn't that poor girl any more, eternally pushed about
from place to place. I had something of my own at last. What more
could you expect me to want? It was an undreamed of situation to
be in.

HERO. Suppose he'd only wanted to amuse himself with you?

LUCILE. That's a risk all girls have to take. One mustn't get too
sentimental over the silly ones.

HERO (*leaning towards her*) All the same, I know the habits of the
animal, when it wants to be loved. Didn't he do almost too much to
make himself interesting?

(LUCILE *smiles, for the first time in agreement with him*)

LUCILE. Yes, almost too much. But I knew what he meant.

HERO. What could you have hoped for, the first time you set eyes
on that jester, that noble mountebank?

LUCILE. No more than the right to be happy in his arms for a
moment, as I was, right away.

HERO. And after that?

LUCILE. After that, if one has to live in the world, the real world,
it's just a matter of earning one's living. There's never any lack of
orphans, and nursemaids will always be needed to look after them.
That doesn't matter. I should have had my moment. (*She sits up*)

HERO. Not even a clinging vine. Good old Tiger. He manages to
avoid everything in the world that's in bad taste. He arrives at the
height of the party: weariness, futility, sickness of soul. Milord lifts
a finger, and behold. An angel appears, who gives herself to him at
once and for ever. For with you it is for ever, isn't it?

LUCILE (*leaning forward*) Oh, yes.

HERO. Oh, yes. And if he kills himself in a car crash on his way
home tonight, you'll die some time tomorrow? Just taking time to
make your little dispositions. Daphnis and Chloe, Dido and Aeneas,
Cadmus and Hermione, let's see, what else? Tristram and Iseult
without even King Mark and that inconvenient sword between you.
One day; milord feels the time is ripe for an idyll. An idyll? Why,
here it is, Monsieur le Comte, on a plate. She is waiting.

LUCILE. That's right. I am waiting.

HERO. All he had to do was appear and there she was, spotless
and eternal. Let others be content with women who live only for

pleasure. For I'm sure you'll never learn that trick, you'll always be as prickly, even when he's bought you a whole wardrobe of new dresses and suddenly everyone's telling you how pretty you are.

LUCILE. He will never buy me dresses, don't you think it.

HERO. Why not?

LUCILE. Because I won't let him. I've acquired the good habit of buying one myself from time to time, and I shan't change it. (*She sits up and puts her book under the pillow*)

HERO. Everything! Everything! (*He rises*) He will have everything. Intelligence, virtue, and altruism thrown in. You are rich; I am poor and proud. Your money might come between us. With a wave of my hand I abolish it. It doesn't exist. (*He turns the chair to face the bed, then crosses to the trunk and sits astride it*) Milord needn't even be embarrassed. I bet you'll insist on staying here to look after his aunt's orphans, like a good girl, and content yourself with leaving your door on the latch for him at night.

LUCILE. No, I couldn't do that. But I shall find another children's home near Paris, and he will come and see me whenever he likes.

HERO. That will be nice! He'll ask politely to see you in the parlour and you'll both shake in your shoes when the matron gives you a lecture. He'll blush like a schoolboy. He'll start wooing you all over again. But there's a slight snag; you don't know our monsieur. He's a typical French gentleman, with centuries of breeding behind him. He'll never agree to let you go on working.

LUCILE. He will have to. Weren't either of you taught that man must earn his bread by the sweat of his brow?

HERO. No. We went to rather distinguished schools, where that formed no part of the curriculum. If they ordered you about, spoke to you rudely, made you watch the clock, Tiger would die of shame, my dear, just that. I know him.

LUCILE. Nobody dies of shame so easily, believe me. Besides, it's not so unpleasant to work—not much more unpleasant than doing nothing. When one sees all the trouble you two have to take, just to kill time.

HERO. Do you know, my dear, it's true. We've sweated all our lives. What courage and ambition we must have had, to stick it out. Look at the poor, on Sunday, see what they do with their time. They drag round the streets, they yawn, they're worn out trying to exist until Monday. We've had them seven days a week, those Sundays. Ever since we were children. (*He rises*) It hasn't been easy for us. But at last we've succeeded. Now the worst part is over. (*He moves to the washstand and refills his glass*) Tiger is a man who manages to amuse himself twelve or fifteen hours a day without fatigue. Now you should learn how to do it. He will teach you.

LUCILE. No.

HERO. But if you spend your life in a children's home, while he's at the races, it will be like the daily woman who married a nightwatchman. You'll never manage to meet. Damn it, you must be sensible. (*He moves to the bed*)

Lucile. I don't want to be sensible. That's the first word one uses when one is going to do something wicked.

Hero. Something wicked? Something "wicked"? Now, that's a word no-one quite knows how to define. In any case, my love, there is something worse, which is to do something stupid.

Lucile. I want to be stupid. That's my own way of loving. Can you see me sitting in a luxurious apartment, for which he pays the rent, waiting for him to arrive with a little parcel dangling on a ribbon? I should hate him at the end of a week. That would be *really* stupid.

Hero. Socrates! You know all the answers. (*He moves down* l) You're going to stop him making a horrible blunder, and he'll accept it joyfully, the hypocrite. Only too delighted to play the little game. He'll buy himself a nice little suit at the Samaritaine and come and wait for you outside your orphanage at six o'clock with a tuppenny bunch of violets. He'll be twenty again, with all the freshness of youth and all his future before him. To be offered that at forty, just when you think you're finished . . . (*He cries out*) Oh, no, it's too much, I tell you.

Lucile. What is the matter?

(Hero, *controls himself, explains calmly with a malicious smile*)

Hero. I tell you it's too much. I'm saying it's too good to be true. (*He moves to the foot of the bed*) A typical fairy story.

(*There is a silence. They look at each other*)

Lucile (*rising and moving to him*) Sir, we've talked for a little while as he wanted us to do. But now it would be kinder of you, perhaps, to let me go to sleep. I have to get up early in the morning for the children.

Hero (*not moving*) We haven't talked for five minutes yet. Do sit down, my love, give me a little while longer. In any case, I shall get less sleep than you will. You can see I'm at a loose end, that I shall die of misery all by myself. Won't you take pity on me, mademoiselle?

(Lucile *sits on the downstage side of the bed*)

(*He moves above the bed*) Besides, there's nothing compromising about me. A girl can allow me in her bedroom without danger quite late at night. Not very appetising either, I know. A wreck. And I'm a year younger than Tiger. Heigh-ho. So much for the life of pleasure. (*He drinks*)

Lucile (*gently*) Why don't you try and drink less?

Hero. Why should I try? I should have to be lucky like milord and meet an angel who will take me under her wing. Angels are rare.

Lucile (*gently*) Perhaps you'll meet one, some day.

Hero (*laughing*) A soak like me? With my drunkard's face, my drunkard's smell? (*He sits on the upstage side of the bed and leans over to her*) Speaking as an angel, do admit that if I'd been the one to court you, you might have deferred my conversion to a later date?

(LUCILE *rises, moves to the trunk and sits on it*)

(*He looks at her and smiles*) Another indiscreet question. (*He rises, moves to the chair, puts it near the washstand and sits*) I'm a bit heavy-handed, I fear. However—when you descended on this house a few days ago, that very first evening at dinner, there wasn't a single man—I except Villebosse, who doesn't count—who looked at anyone but you. Now, doesn't that mean something?

LUCILE (*a little astonished*) All the men?

HERO. Isn't she sweet? She didn't even notice. Yes, my dear, there were three of us. The butler's too old, but Tiger's footman got all the forks mixed up when he was serving. Now, there's a lad who was burning to be converted, like the rest of us. Plain as a pikestaff.

LUCILE (*rising*) Please—that's enough.

HERO (*rising*) Why? Have I hurt your feelings? Have you still got old-fashioned class-prejudices, my love? The boy sleeps in the west wing, too; if I were you, I'd lock—(*he moves to the door and closes it*) and bolt my door at night. We all know he's the son of the grandfather's first footman, but still, he was a paratrooper in the war, and that's an adventure that shook new ideas into people like him. What would you have done had it been he—or perhaps myself—instead of Tiger, who said: "I want you"?

LUCILE (*with a step towards him; radiant*) But, sir, Tiger's the one I love.

HERO (*after a pause*) You do take the wind out of one's sails. What else can I suggest?

LUCILE (*turning away to face front; gently*) Nothing.

HERO. Shall we play at Let's Pretend? Just for a moment or two? Just a little game to kill this long evening that frightens me so much? (*He puts his glass on the washstand*) Now: Tiger hasn't said a word to you: you don't love Tiger. For a week I've watched you quietly, through every meal, and tonight I've made an excuse to come to your room and—(*he moves to the end of the bed*) tell you, as he did, that I want you.

LUCILE. That's a game I refuse to play. It would be dreadful. If he found out that this was the way you were spending the evening, what would he think?

HERO. You ought to know we've exchanged quite a few mistresses, Tiger and I, as all good friends do. (*He moves* C) Besides, it would only be tit for tat. There has been an angel in my life, mademoiselle, I was lying to you. A very long time ago. I was nineteen and in those days I hadn't taken to the bottle.

LUCILE (*stammering*) And he . . .

HERO. No. He didn't steal her. But he made me leave her for reasons which seemed to me valid enough at the time. She married someone else, who made her very unhappy and now she's dead. And it was that brief episode, that short broken engagement, which has turned me into what I am.

LUCILE (*softly*) How horrible.

HERO (*coldly*) Yes. Horrible, as you say. But Tiger owes me a girl now, in exchange. And that's why I am in your bedroom tonight.

LUCILE (*retreating* R; *pale*) Go away, or I'll call for help.

HERO. There's no-one to call to. Besides, if that's what frightens you, set your heart at rest. I won't touch you. (*He moves to her*) I only want to talk to you.

(*They look at each other, standing face to face*)

LUCILE (*crying out suddenly*) I love him. I won't listen to you. (*She backs to the wall* R)

(HERO *moves to her, puts his hands on the wall either side of her and leans over her*)

HERO (*sweetly*) You will, my love.

LUCILE. I'll stop up my ears.

HERO. Ah, but it's so fascinating to listen to one's death sentence.

LUCILE. I'm not interested in your drunken, neurotic complications. I'm young and I'm sane and I love him.

(HERO *moves to the bed and lolls on it*)

You'll be ashamed of this ugly scene tomorrow. Go back to your own room.

HERO. Dear child, I am never ashamed.

LUCILE. Are you such a good friend of his wife? Besides, you know she doesn't love him. So what difference does it make to you if we love each other? I'm not asking him to marry me—not even to go away with me. I'll stay out of sight. He can go on leading his own life, in his own world, if that's what frightens you all so much. I'm only asking you not to stop us loving each other.

HERO (*sneering*) His own life, his own world? What do you take me for? Papa Duval with his tophat in *La Dame aux Camelias?* It doesn't matter a damn to me.

LUCILE. Then what have you been doing ever since you came into this room? Do you think I didn't understand what was behind every word you said, even when you pretended to be fond of him and to take pity on me? Why go to so much trouble to try and destroy something which may be true and good, and asks nothing but the right to exist? Because you hate it?

HERO. Not even that.

LUCILE. Then why?

HERO (*in a murmur*) I like to break things. (*He rises and moves to the washstand*)

(LUCILE, *erect and calm, looks at him.* HERO *tries to meet her gaze for a long moment, then suddenly pours out a drink and swallows it at a gulp*)

LUCILE (*gently*) Poor Hero. Poor little monster. (*She crosses to him*) You don't frighten me any more. How unhappy you must be with that load on your back.

HERO (*shouting suddenly*) If I'm unhappy, it's my own concern. (*He moves down* L) Mind your own business.

LUCILE (*moving down* LC) It is my business. You're trying to hurt me, even now. And all I can feel for you is pity.

HERO (*crossing above Lucile to* R *of her; shouting*) I forbid you to pity me. Poor miserable little nobody of a schoolmarm with your tiny clean hands and feet, in your tuppenny-ha'penny gown, with your principles, your high-mindedness, your thrift. You're what I hate most in the world. What I find most stupid, most fatuous. I'd rather have a whore with an enticing belly; a tart who makes you pay every time and betrays you just the same. I'd rather have a vice-ridden hag who stuffs cocaine up her nose, a drunken tramp wallowing in her own filth under a bridge. I loathe you. And I forbid you to look at me like that. (*He crosses above Lucile to* L *of her, barely concealing his malicious joy*) Do you really want to know where Tiger is tonight? (*He crosses above Lucile to* R *of her*) Do you know what was in the telegram that called him away so abruptly? (*He crosses above Lucile to* L *of her*) Do you know what message he gave me for you?

(LUCILE *retreats below the bed to* R, *with her hands to her mouth*)

LUCILE (*crying out*) It isn't true!

HERO. What isn't true? I haven't said anything yet. (*He looks at her slyly*) Not even brave, either. I expect you cry out like that when you go to the dentist. I can just see you, even before he's reached for the drill. She looks down her nose at you, she thinks she is Joan of Arc, Antigone, and the rest of them—all the heroines in her dear little school books; then when the moment arrives——

(LUCILE *fumbles for her handkerchief in her dressing-gown pocket*)

—out comes the little handkerchief——

(LUCILE *snatches her hand from her pocket and moves* R, *above the trunk*)

—the little sobs, the little tears, she's no better than anybody else. She doesn't even know how to control herself. And she has the impudence to judge you, she dares to pity you.

LUCILE (*turning to face him*) You're a monster!

HERO (*leaning on the door lintel*) What did I tell you? You try to be tactful. You observe the conventions. You choke yourself telling her she's charming, she's desirable, and you're quite ready to console her—you or the valet. And that's all the thanks you get. (*He cries suddenly*) Come along, have hysterics—I shan't go on till you've finished.

LUCILE (*stiffening*) I'm not going to cry.

HERO. Good. I prefer that. I have a horror of tears. They make me sick. You're really beautiful at this moment. A small quivering animal cornered by the hounds, at bay, back to the wall. One would have to be as stupid as those two female parrots not to agree.

The little poisoner of the house, the little intruder who must be shown the door. The little skeleton at the feast.

LUCILE (*crying out*) Say what you have to say.

HERO (*moving LC; smiling*) You realize he's already rather late? We have plenty of time. The butler and the cook are getting drunk in the pantry and I've packed the paratrooper off to do the same in the next village. All the others are shut up in their rooms, miles away in the other wing, wondering what's going to happen next. I can see them tossing on their beds. Monsieur Damiens, smooth as a dark crow who's lost his piece of cheese; Hortensia and the Countess, with detective stories and sleeping pills within reach. But sleep stays away. What about the little plotter in her attic in the west wing, cooking up God knows what against the family concord and the approved liaisons. Won't someone manage to get rid of her at last? (*He moves above the bed*) My dear, Tiger has suddenly realized, too late, that he has made a great mistake, the sort of mistake only he can make. If he had asked my advice beforehand, I would have told him to spare you this unhappiness. You were a virgin, virginity was your meagre capital—he should never have touched it. (*He moves down c*) Besides, there's something about you. I would have said to him, "You can do as you please with a chambermaid, that goes without saying: if you don't have her, the footman will, either today or the day after." You're worth more than that: I admit it. But don't be too angry with him, all the same. He isn't wicked. He's a sentimentalist, an incurable sentimentalist, and it goes to his head —that's all. Besides, he has every excuse. It's so adorable, a new little being nestling in your arms, saying she loves you, that she belongs to you for ever. For ever—for him that meant tonight—the here and now. (*He moves to her*) It was a brand-new pleasure for him, something he's never known before. He'd have had to be very high-minded to tear his arms away, to say no. And besides, as you've just told me, it's a risk all girls have to run. (*He moves LC*) After all, if they ask for it . . . The trouble is that next morning, you find the little one still loves you. "For ever", so far as she's concerned, begins with breakfast. And now you have to start worrying about her. She's deep in confidences already. The little darling, head on your shoulder, has already started to prattle about her old mother, who's so lonely, to whom one must be so very kind—of the little dishes she cooks so nicely, the name she's going to give her first baby. (*He moves c*) It's all gone, the unique joy of the night before, your sacrificial faun: hey presto! You're carrying the slop-pail for the entire family. You can see yourself, already, pushing the pram. A free translation, of course. I know that you were sensible and discreet. (*He moves to her*) "I'll go on working just the same: he'll never buy me anything: we shall be free: nothing will matter but our love." Shall I tell you the whole truth, my dear? Yes. You're strong enough to bear it now. That's what frightened Tiger. He would rather you'd asked him for a mink coat and a nicely furnished little flat. (*He moves above the bed*) To have a nice little mistress, in a life like his, that fits in very nicely. (*He moves to the foot of the bed*) A great unselfish love—that is beyond price.

LUCILE. Why didn't he tell me himself?

HERO. Why should you make a hero out of that likeable play-boy? He knows, like all of us, ever since Napoleon gave us the tip, that there's only one cure for love—flight. He has flown.

LUCILE (*stammering*) Then why did he tell me he loved me?

HERO. Emotion—fascination—contagion: love is as catching as influenza. A certain natural eloquence, too. You are young. You'll find other men. (*He moves* L) Beware of the sentimentalists, my faun, they're the worst.

LUCILE (*after a pause; stiffly*) Is that all he asked you to say to me.

HERO. No, of course not. He's a gentleman. First of all, a cheque —(*he puts his hands in his pocket*)

(LUCILE *recoils*)

—which you refuse, of course. I'm with you, there; I think it's clumsy. I shouldn't even have mentioned it, but after all, I'm only a messenger. Then, as I told you just now, he said: "Talk to her a little. You might try to comfort her . . ."

(LUCILE *resists a moment, restraining herself, then suddenly falls sobbing on the bed*)

There. My little cardboard heroine. Let yourself go. It's better to cry. (*He moves above the bed and talks gently to her, almost like a mother*) She draws herself up, plays the proud beauty, wants to behave like a real lady. Yesterday, she was still playing with her dolls, and at the first little disappointment, she ran away to hide in her mamma's skirts. Only now—no mamma any more. She's grown-up, she's all alone. She has no-one but the horrid godfather, the dry-as-dust lawyer, who has put on grandmother's pretty bonnet over his ugly wolf's head—all the better to eat you with, my dear. Ah, how lonely it can be, can't it, my kitten? I know all about that. You, who were a little sorry for me not so long ago, now do you understand? (*He sits on the bed, rolls her over, looks for a moment at her face, then rolls her back and reaches for the filled glass on the right end of the washstand*) There. Now she's going to have a drink. Like a good little girl. (*He makes her drink, supporting her head*) Then she'll have another, and another. She will have understood, yes, she will. (*He holds her against his shoulder. He is not acting, he is crying as he murmurs*) Evangeline. (*He pauses and holds Lucile to him, stroking her gently. He murmurs, looking away into the distance*) My darling, my poor darling. Life is ugly, isn't it? She was raring to go—believed in everything, and suddenly there she was with life yawning like an abyss in front of her. She didn't say a word—she hid away so she could cry in peace, and then she married an ugly old banker the family had found for her. A beast in her bed at night, and all day the drudgery of parading up and down for his pleasure, covered in jewels. So she cries in secret for two or three years, very quietly, and then one fine day, when she's too tired, she dies—that's all, without a word, without leaving any more trace of her passing than the flight of a bird through the air. (*He is crying. He caresses her. She is lying against his shoulder. He murmurs, his face bathed in tears*) My child. My darling child. My poor little lost child.

HERO *holds* LUCILE *in his arms. She lets herself go. He puts his arm over her and lies on the bed as—*

the CURTAIN *falls*

SCENE 2

SCENE—*The Salon. The following morning.*

When the CURTAIN *rises, the settee is up* RC *and the armchair up* LC. VILLEBOSSE, *alone, is crossing up* R *to up* L, *furious, with his mind made up, we do not yet know to what. The* COUNT, *carrying his prompt script, enters down* R *and crosses to* RC. *The* FOOTMAN *follows him on, kneels beside the Count and buckles the Count's knee breeches.*

COUNT. Here already, Villebosse? I'm late—I got home in the small hours. Forgive me for imposing a morning rehearsal on you all, but this afternoon I shall be saddled with the orchestra. I must settle the music.

VILLEBOSSE (*crossing to* L *of the Count*) Sir—I've been waiting for you for an hour. It was impossible for me to speak to you alone yesterday, and I must have a serious talk with you.

(*The* COUNT *signs to the Footman to leave.*
The FOOTMAN *rises and exits down* R)

You seem very cheerful, sir, very happy.

COUNT (*crossing and putting his script on the table down* L) Most cheerful, Villebosse, and most happy. (*He moves to the armchair* LC *and sits*) As I have never been before.

VILLEBOSSE (*moving behind the settee*) You have all the luck. Other people have none, sir. Other people suffer. Other people haven't the same reasons for rejoicing as you have, sir.

COUNT. I should hope not. For once in my life, my motives are extremely personal. Until this moment, I've been weak enough to take my pleasures in company. Now it dawns on me that happiness is a solitary exercise.

VILLEBOSSE. Is there some double meaning behind your words, sir?

COUNT. Since the invention of language, Villebosse, there has always been some double meaning behind the spoken word. In fact, words were invented expressly for that reason.

VILLEBOSSE. If there were a double meaning, sir, it would be out of place. The situation in which we find ourselves is very delicate —that should never be forgotten.

COUNT. My dear boy, it's never cost me a wink of sleep. Still, you've chosen a bad moment to bring it up, because I have decided to forget it completely.

VILLEBOSSE. What do you mean by that, sir?

COUNT. That I find you a most remarkable young man. I am charmed to have you for my wife's lover.

VILLEBOSSE. Sir, I forbid you to trifle with the lady's honour. Withdraw that word, sir, withdraw it. Or you shall give me satis-faction.

COUNT. What word?

VILLEBOSSE. The word you have just pronounced, sir. Your cynicism is a detestable pose. I will not permit it to degrade a being who has the right to our respect. The Countess, sir, is above all suspicion.

COUNT. But devil take it, Villebosse, what suspicion?

VILLEBOSSE. Sir, you understood me perfectly. Don't try to make me repeat an expression I find offensive. If you consider yourself authorized to bellow out right and left that your wife is having a love affair, you'll have to answer to me, sir.

COUNT. Villebosse, you're adorable! I never tire of listening to you and watching you evolve. You are the funniest man I've ever known.

VILLEBOSSE (*moving in front of the settee*) I am suffering, sir, nothing more. I am sincere by nature.

COUNT. So I see.

VILLEBOSSE (*sitting on the settee, at the right end of it*) No matter what I do, I shall never get used to the corruption of the degenerate little world in which you live. I come from Carcassonne, where we are simple squires. My family home has kept its moat and drawbridge since the thirteenth century. We've never budged from there, we've never put in central heating, and we've never made jokes about the honour of our wives. When I knew I loved the Countess, I came and suggested to you that we should fight to the death. It was quite simple. Either I would marry the widow, or disappear. You refused.

COUNT. I wasn't ready to die that morning. Nor to kill you, either. I like you very much, Villebosse.

VILLEBOSSE. You wanted it, this complex and degrading state of things.

COUNT. I wanted to live. That's always complex and degrading.

VILLEBOSSE (*rising*) It can't be altered now. Here then, sir, is what I have to tell you—sir—the honour and happiness of the Countess concern me personally. I will not allow you to be unfaithful to your wife.

COUNT. What!

VILLEBOSSE. You understood me perfectly. I will not tolerate you making her ridiculous, as you are doing, for the sake of a nobody.

You will behave yourself, sir, from now on. Either you will behave yourself or answer for it to me.

COUNT. What are your demands, Villebosse?

VILLEBOSSE (*crossing above the Count to* L *of him*) You must break with this young person immediately. Return to the conjugal hearth. The Countess agrees to wipe the slate clean, she will forget and forgive.

COUNT. Must I break with Hortensia, too?

VILLEBOSSE (*moving down* L) She puts up with her. It's one of her weaknesses. (*He crosses to* R) She has always indulged you in a manner I fail to understand. Just be discreet, show the Countess more attention at all times than you do the other lady: give her precedence always. Devil take it! It's strange that it should be my business to remind you—she is your wife, sir.

COUNT. Villebosse, I love you more and more. (*He rises and crosses to Villebosse*) Let me embrace you.

VILLEBOSSE (*backing down* R) No.

COUNT (*following him*) Why not? I'm sure you're very fond of me, too.

VILLEBOSSE. It would be most irregular. Keep your distance, sir. Our situation is too delicate. But never forget, I've got my eye on you.

(*The* COUNTESS *enters down* L *and crosses to* C)

COUNTESS (*as she enters*) When I think, Tiger, that you've succeeded in getting us all up at ten o'clock . . . But I declare, the dawn is ravishing. (*She moves to the armchair and turns*) We really should get up earlier. What a glorious morning. Did you have a good night?

COUNT. Yes, Eliane. (*He moves up* L) May I have a word with you?

COUNTESS. Villebosse?

VILLEBOSSE (*moving* RC) Dearest Eliane?

COUNTESS (*crossing to Villebosse*) Would you like to make yourself useful?

VILLEBOSSE (*drunk with devotion*) Always.

COUNTESS. Run round all the rooms and pull out the slackers. We start rehearsing in ten minutes' time.

VILLEBOSSE (*crossing to the door down* L) Leave it to me, Eliane, in ten minutes everyone will be here. (*He blows a kiss to the Countess*)

(*The* COUNTESS *blows a kiss to Villebosse. The* COUNT *also blows a kiss to Villebosse.*

VILLEBOSSE *exits down* L. *The* COUNTESS *crosses and closes the door behind him, then turns to the Count*)

COUNTESS. I'm listening.

COUNT (*moving down* L) I'll try to be brief. But you're a clever woman, Eliane, and I know you'll understand.

COUNTESS. What a portentous beginning. (*She takes a cigarette from the box on the table down* L, *and lights it*)

COUNT. Yes. I am in love with that girl.

COUNTESS. Very well.

COUNT. We've had an intelligent life together, Eliane: we've shared a mutual horror of melodrama, not because it frightens us, but because it seems to us in bad taste. You've turned a blind eye to my mistresses, and I have never asked whom you invite to tea.

(*The* COUNTESS *moves above the armchair*)

We have given some superb parties, our house is one of the few people really enjoy visiting and, considering what most ordinary marriages are like, ours—to put the thing in a nutshell—has been delightful.

COUNTESS (*moving to the Count*) Thank you, Tiger. (*She kisses him*)

COUNT. No. It's for me to thank you. I was an impossible young man, far too spoiled. We owe our success to your marvellous understanding of life.

(*The* COUNTESS *sits in the armchair*)

In a vociferous world, where sex is on public show and hearts grow heavier and heavier, we have kept our inward gaiety. We have lived like dancers, matching our steps to music.

COUNTESS (*looking away*) And none of that attracts you any more?

COUNT. It will always seem to me the only intelligent way to live. The only way of escaping muddle and vulgarity. Only . . .

COUNTESS. Only what?

COUNT. That line of my life, so graceful and so well-defined, running from my first successful ball to my probable Presidency of the Jockey Club in twenty years' time, and to my funeral at the Madeleine with all my friends in top-hats—I am beginning to realize that though it would doubtless be a pretty memory for others, a delightful theme for an article in the *Figaro*—it meant nothing to me. I did not know why I was so gay all the time: I was bored.

COUNTESS. And it's that child, up in her attic, who has made you understand.

COUNT. Yes. You have too much taste, I know, Eliane, not to spare me a description of my feelings. I love her. I never knew exactly what that meant. It's stupid, it has no verve; it's graceless, it's unfunny; it has none of those qualities I thought I prized so much— (*he sits on the settee*) but it's love.

COUNTESS (*rising and crossing above the settee to* R *of it*) Is it so new, Tiger? I have seen you on the verge of suicide two or three times, when girls have resisted you.

COUNT. I couldn't bear to have my desires thwarted. Everything I wanted badly enough, I had to have at once. This time, I'm not even in that kind of hurry. My greatest joy is to be with her—nothing else matters—but if you asked me to wait, Eliane, for one reason or another—I could wait: for a long time; without growing tired.

COUNTESS. I won't take you at your word. It would be too sad if you tried it, and lost this fine new confidence. (*She crosses below the settee to the mirror*) You know I've never stopped you taking your pleasure?

COUNT. My poor Eliane, we're no longer speaking the same language. This time, there's no question of taking.

COUNTESS. I see. (*She moves below the armchair*) Then what is in question?

COUNT (*rising; gently*) Giving.

COUNTESS. You've got time, you've money in your pocket. Give, my dear boy, give. What's stopping you? Take a little trip with her, buy her some new frocks. You've been saying for ten years that you wanted to go to Japan. Take her to Venice and hide your amours there—I'll tell our friends you've gone to Japan.

COUNT. My poor Eliane, I'm going much farther away than Tokio.

COUNTESS. That's the second time you've used a word I abominate. I am not your poor Eliane. Do you want us to separate, Tiger, so you can marry her?

COUNT (*moving* RC) Why should we upset your uncle the bishop with a divorce—have a civil servant meddling with our affairs again? It seems quite unnecessary.

COUNTESS. She hasn't asked you yet? She will within a week. These little persons, who give themselves to the first comers in their attics, have a passion for respectability.

COUNT. That is the only separation I fear, Eliane. That in your anger and spite you may use the wrong word. I have always esteemed and admired you. There is already an emerald between us: let's not add anything else. (*He crosses to her*)

COUNTESS (*smoothing his cravat*) Let me get this quite clear. We give the entertainment as arranged, and the next day you leave me for as long as you love that child, for as long as she loves you? Very well, I agree. And, as you see, I'm not too worried. Enjoy yourself, Tiger, you can tell me all about it when you return.

(HORTENSIA *enters down* R)

(*She crosses to Hortensia and kisses her*) Ah! Hortensia! So good, so tender, so trustful.

(*The* COUNT *crosses up* L)

Men are worthless creatures.

(HORTENSIA *crosses below the Countess to the table down* L.
      HERO *enters, glass in hand, down* R. *He seems a little absent*)

Hero, my little Hero, you look very depressed. Hero, you're being unreasonable again. Put down that glass—it's too early to drink.

HERO. No. (*He sits on the chair down* R)

(VILLEBOSSE *enters down* R)

VILLEBOSSE (*to the Countess, indicating Hero*) He's abominably drunk, he can't even talk clearly. I defy you to rehearse with him. (*He moves up* R *and gazes out of the window*) As for the girl and Damiens, they aren't in their rooms.

COUNTESS (*moving behind the settee*) Tiger, you're the only one who can find them. Will you go up, please, and bring them down?

(*The* COUNT *crosses towards the door down* L.

DAMIENS *enters suddenly down* L, *wearing street clothes, black and strange*)

DAMIENS. I beg you to forgive me, Madame la Comtesse. But most regretfully, I shall have to resign my part and leave the château.

(*The* COUNT *stops, turns and moves to* L *of Damiens*)

COUNTESS. What are you saying, Monsieur Damiens? We're giving the performance the day after tomorrow.

DAMIENS. My goddaughter left for the station very early this morning, on foot and alone. This impulsive action can only be a consequence of yesterday's unhappy contretemps. After so painful an incident, I could not think of staying, either.

COUNT (*white-faced*) How do you know she's gone?

DAMIENS. When I went to her room to fetch her just now—(*he takes a letter from his pocket*) I found this note for you on her table, Monsieur le Comte. (*He hands the letter to the Count*) And there was another for me. (*He moves to the window up* L *and gazes out*)

(*The* COUNT *opens the letter*)

COUNTESS. Oh, come now, Damiens, you're dreaming. We had a very friendly chat together last night, the matter was entirely closed.

(*The* COUNT, *who is turned to stone, letter in hand, murmurs as in a dream*)

COUNT. "You were right. It was impossible. I am going away. I shall never see you again."

(*A silence falls on everyone. The* COUNTESS *moves behind the settee, looking triumphantly at the Count*)

HERO. Is that all?

(*They look at the* COUNT, *who does not answer and gazes into the distance, pale as death*)

COUNTESS (*turning to Damiens*) It's quite extraordinary. Monsieur Damiens, you who knew her . . .

DAMIENS (*turning to the Countess*) Forgive me, madame, my train leaves in a few minutes, I have only just time to get to the station. Her letter tells me nothing more, apart from her determination never to see me again, either. There's no doubt she was deeply hurt,

far more seriously than we thought. Now she's gone, God alone
knows where, all alone and heartbroken, without shelter, without
money—nothing.

COUNTESS. Good Heavens! We never gave her her six months'.
wages.

(*The* COUNT, *who has stood silent, motionless, as if struck by light-
ning, suddenly rushes out down* R)

HORTENSIA (*crossing to* LC; *crying out*) Tiger, where are you going?
COUNTESS. To get his car and search the roads. But which roads?
Run after him, Damiens, he can drop you at the station.
DAMIENS (*crossing quickly to the door down* R) Good-bye, madame.

(DAMIENS *exits down* R. VILLEBOSSE *crosses to the windows up* L)

COUNTESS (*moving to Hortensia*) The child must have taken the
five o'clock bus for Alençon. (*She moves down* R) She'll have caught
her connection there already. Tiger will never know which way
she's gone. He has no hope whatsoever of finding her.
HORTENSIA. She may change her mind—write to him . . .
COUNTESS. Don't you believe it. (*She moves to* R *of Hortensia*) Now
we're free to say it, she had got a certain integrity. Her very depar-
ture proves it. She loved him—of course she did. (*She moves to* L *of
Hero*) That's why we need have no fear. After what has happened,
she'll never try to see him again.
HORTENSIA (*moving* C; *suddenly gentle*) But what will Tiger do?
COUNTESS (*looking at Hortensia; genuinely astonished*) What a kind
soul you are, Hortensia, kind to a fault. He'll be miserable for a
month or two and then he'll start enjoying himself again. Our first
guests will be here this evening. For two days, no matter how
wretched he is, he'll be unable to think of anything but his entertainment. (*She moves to Hortensia*) Come, my dear, let's have some
breakfast. All this has given me quite an appetite.
HORTENSIA. What about the part?
COUNTESS (*crossing to the door down* R) I had foreseen the con-
tingency. Tiger gave the part to Leonor in the first place, and she's
word-perfect still. (*She turns*) She's taken the plane for Le Mans and
I've sent the Renault to meet her. She'll be here in an hour. (*She
moves* RC) And I'll ring up Gontaut-Biron, he must be over his flu
by this time.
HORTENSIA (*moving to the Countess*) What? You've sent for Leonor?
After what you told me about her and Tiger?
COUNTESS. My dear girl, I'm very fond of you, but I'm afraid
you don't fully grasp the situation. Our first care must be to comfort
Tiger. Either I don't know him at all, or within a week he'll be
thinking of nothing but Leonor. It stirs him to frenzy when people
resist him. Come along and have some coffee. We both need it.

(*The* COUNTESS *exits down* R.
HORTENSIA *follows her off*)

E

VILLEBOSSE (*crossing down* R *and calling after the Countess*) Eliane, I've had no breakfast, either. (*He shrugs and crosses to* L)

(HERO, *still abstracted and glass in hand, calls Villebosse back*)

HERO (*in a thick voice*) Sir.
VILLEBOSSE (*stopping*) Sir?
HERO. One moment, if you please.

(VILLEBOSSE *turns, surprised*)

I believe you're an excellent shot, sir?
VILLEBOSSE (*moving to the armchair*) What do you mean by that, sir?
HERO (*rising and moving to* L *of the settee*) I would even go so far as to say I believe you've won several international pistol championships? (*He sits on the settee*)
VILLEBOSSE. That is correct.
HERO. Well, sir, I have the honour to tell you you are not loved as you would like to believe.
VILLEBOSSE. What, sir?
HERO. One is never loved as one would like to believe, that is a universal truth. But for you, there is a more particular truth. Since yesterday evening you have been, sir—to use a word that revolts me —a cuckold.
VILLEBOSSE. You're drunk, sir! Withdraw the word.
HERO. I am drunk. But when I'm drunk I have all my wits about me. I repeat the word. It is exact. I was not in my own room last night. I was elsewhere. You understand me, Villebosse?
VILLEBOSSE (*advancing on him; terrible*) What? Do you realize what you are daring to insinuate, sir?
HERO. It seems obvious to me. Don't make me repeat an indelicate word.
VILLEBOSSE. Very well, sir. You have at least the merit of frankness. I've suspected for some time that you were trying to pick a quarrel with me. We will fight. Just give me time to change my clothes.
HERO (*still seated*) Please hurry. I wish it to be now. I shall be waiting on the terrace.
VILLEBOSSE. At your service, sir. I'm as much in a hurry as you are. (*He turns towards the door down* L)
HERO. Sir.
VILLEBOSSE (*stopping and turning*) Sir?
HERO. To regularize the position, strike me.
VILLEBOSSE. Sir, it isn't necessary.
HERO. Sir, it is. If you don't slap my face, I won't fight.
VILLEBOSSE. But we've already agreed to meet, sir. I give you the choice of arms, if that's what's worrying you.
HERO. It's my privilege only if you strike me. I know the rules. Strike me at once, sir—(*he rises and cries out*) or dear God, I'll throw my glass in your face,

(VILLEBOSSE *moves down* L *and faces front*)

Villebosse, I want you to. And hard. I want to feel it. Dear God—
you dirty cuckold. I tell you, you must.

VILLEBOSSE (*crossing to Hero*) Oh, very well—you preposterous
creature. Really—(*he slaps Hero's face*) it's too absurd.

HERO (*pale, motionless and erect*) No. It's quite correct. (*He lifts
a finger*) I choose pistols.

VILLEBOSSE *bows, stiff and a little surprised at the choice, then exits
down* L. HERO *is left alone, motionless, lost in a dream. He slowly
empties his glass and as he lowers it from his mouth—*

the CURTAIN *falls*

FURNITURE AND PROPERTY LIST

ACT I

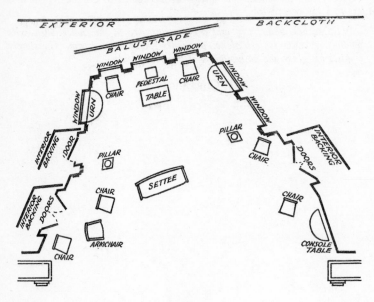

SCENE 1

On stage: 2 upright chairs (down R)
              Armchair (down R)
              Low stone urn with climbing plant (R)
              High pedestal (up C) *On it:* large vase with ferns, etc.
              Low stone urn with vine (L)
              Upright chair (up R) *On it:* tray with 2 plain glass wine glasses,
                  3 coloured wine glasses, decanter of brandy, decanter of
                  sherry, ashtray, with cigarettes, matches
              Upright chair (up LC)
              Console table (down L) *On it:* 4 small paper-covered scripts,
                  ashtray, matches
              Mirror (on wall down L)
              Table (up C) *On it:* upright chair, prompt script
              Settee. *On it:* dust cover

Off stage: Upright chair (FOOTMAN)
              Rose (COUNTESS)
               Script (HORTENSIA)
               Script (LUCILE)

Personal: DAMIENS: script
          COUNT: lighter

SCENE 2

Strike: Wigs from table down L and from under vine up L

Reset: Armchair down RC, in line with door down R and facing down R
          Upright chair from down R to above door down R

Off stage: Glass of brandy (HERO)

Personal: COUNT: watch

ACT II

Strike: Script from settee
          Prompt script from table L
          Dirty glasses

Reset: Armchair to RC
          Settee to LC, up and down stage
          Cigarette box from table up C to table L

Set: Clean glasses on tray up C
          Box of cigars on tray
          Fan on table up C

Off stage: Door key (LUCILE)
          Ring (COUNT)

Personal: COUNT: handkerchief

ACT III

SCENE I

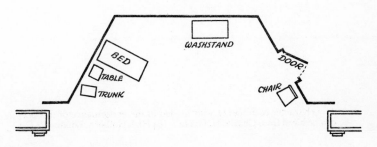

On stage: Bed with bedding. *On it:* paper-covered book
Old trunk on its side with a dress flung over it
Washstand. *On it:* jug, basin, soap dish, toothbrush dish, carafe
and glass, towel on rail at side, oil lamp
On back of door: dress and coat
Small wood chair (down L) *On it:* paper-covered book
Bedside table. *On it:* oil lamp
On floor beside bed: Lucile's slippers

Off stage: Decanter without stopper and half-filled with brandy, 2 glasses
(HERO)

SCENE 2

Set: Settee up RC, facing down L
Armchair up LC, facing down R

Off stage: Letter (DAMIENS)

Any character costumes or wigs needed in the performance of this play
can be hired from Charles H. Fox Ltd, 184 High Holborn, London W.C.1

LIGHTING PLOT

Property fittings required: 2 oil lamps

ACT I, SCENE 1. Interior. A Salon

>THE MAIN ACTING AREAS cover the whole stage

>THE APPARENT SOURCES OF LIGHT are windows up R, up C and up L

To open: Effect of spring sunshine
No cues

ACT I, SCENE 2. The Salon

To open: Lights as Scene 1
No cues

ACT II. The Salon

To open: Lights as Act I
No cues

ACT III, SCENE 1. Interior. An attic. Night

>THE MAIN ACTING AREAS cover the whole room

>THE APPARENT SOURCES OF LIGHT are oil lamps down R and up LC

To open: Lamps on
No cues

ACT III, SCENE 2. The Salon

To open: Effect of morning sunshine
No cues

Printed in Great Britain by
Latimer, Trend & Co. Ltd., Whitstable